Illuminating the Dead Sea Scrolls

Illuminating the Dead Sea Scrolls

Mysteries of Qumran Revealed

Donald W. Parry

NEAL A. MAXWELL INSTITUTE *for* RELIGIOUS SCHOLARSHIP

Maxwell Institute Press
Brigham Young University
Provo, Utah

Illuminating the Dead Sea Scrolls:
Mysteries of Qumran Revealed
Donald W. Parry

Cover design: Brad Norr
Book design: Justin Kelly
Art permissions: Alicia M. Hill
Cover art: Interior of Qumran Cave 4.
Frontispiece: The Dead Sea, facing south, showing the western shore where the Qumran caves are located.

Maxwell Institute Press, an imprint of
Neal A. Maxwell Institute for Religious Scholarship
Brigham Young University
Provo, UT 84602
Printed in the United States of America

ISBN 978-0-8425-2854-2

Contents

Introduction

When I was a teenager growing up in the small farming community of Melba, Idaho, in the United States, I was very interested in the Dead Sea Scrolls. Over a period of a few years I collected a few popularized articles on the scrolls and kept them in a file folder for easy access. I had no idea at the time that academic articles existed; even if I did, I would not have comprehended their contents. I enjoyed this little file of articles until I loaned it to a friend from a neighboring town; she was writing an article about the scrolls for a high school research paper. I never saw those articles again. I have sometimes wondered whether or not her teacher was pleased with the outcome of her paper.

Decades later, I continue to demonstrate interest in the scrolls, but now at a much more advanced level. In January 1994, Professor Emanuel Tov, editor in chief of the *Discoveries in the Judaean Desert* series, invited me to participate with the International Team of Translators of the Dead Sea Scrolls. Like other professors in the field, I research and write about the scrolls, present papers at symposia and congresses, and then publish my findings in journals, encyclopedias, and books. Furthermore, I present introductory matters to various lay audiences of different faiths and religions, and I have published books and articles on the scrolls and have made scores of presentations to both academic and popular audiences.

Now my file cabinets are filled to capacity with academic articles about the scrolls, and I have a personal library crammed with books on the topic. I teach various courses on the scrolls to students of Hebrew, everything from introductory courses to advanced courses in which we read the Isaiah or Samuel scrolls in Hebrew. Over the years I have been so involved in the Dead Sea Scrolls that one of my children gave me a personalized license plate to put on my car; it reads DSSCRL (signifying *Dead Sea Scrolls*).

The study and research of the scrolls fires my soul with enthusiasm. I enjoy gaining new insights and understandings of all things ancient. Likewise, I appreciate the opportunity to work with colleagues throughout the world. Those of us in the field of Dead Sea Scrolls studies are a relatively small group of friends and colleagues who are bound together by the common goal of researching the scrolls. I truly appreciate the collegiality and friendship of these scholars who are located in many countries throughout the world. I have coauthored or coedited books with these scholars, shared ideas over dinner, and networked with them. I have also written articles in their honor that appear in published volumes dedicated to their fine scholarship.

Over the years, I have learned that the Dead Sea Scrolls build bridges of good will. Since their discovery in 1947, scholars and popular audiences from various organizations, groups, and religious communities have gathered together to benefit from these remarkable texts. For example, participants of symposia that deal with the scrolls include adherents of Judaism, various Christian denominations, Islam, and other religions and faiths. Likewise, museum exhibits of scrolls draw tens of thousands of visitors from all walks of life and from a range of societal, cultural, and religious backgrounds—all brought together because of a collection of ancient scrolls.

This volume, not meant to be comprehensive, introduces several brief features and characteristics of the Dead Sea Scrolls. A complete assessment of the scrolls would fill multiple volumes of works. My intent is simple—to provide readers a glimpse into the richness and significance of the scrolls. This volume consists of seven chapters, which in turn include fifty-two brief sections.

In preparing this volume, I employed the following sources, all of which are established, standard works on the topic of the Dead Sea Scrolls:

- Martin Abegg Jr., Peter Flint, and Eugene Ulrich, trans. *The Dead Sea Scrolls Bible.* San Francisco: Harper Collins, 1999.
- *Discoveries in the Judaean Desert* (DJD). 40 vols. Oxford: Clarendon Press, 1968–2001.
- Lawrence H. Schiffman and James C. VanderKam, eds. *Encyclopedia of the Dead Sea Scrolls.* Oxford: Oxford University Press, 2000.
- Geza Vermes, trans. *The Complete Dead Sea Scrolls in English.* New York: Penguin Press, 1997.

Professor Emanuel Tov on the right with Donald Parry in Tov's university office (Jerusalem, January 1994).

Donald Parry privately studying the Great Isaiah Scroll in the scrollery of The Israel Museum, Jerusalem.

Acknowledgments

For the creation of this publication I am indebted to many individuals from the Neal A. Maxwell Institute for Religious Scholarship, Brigham Young University: Joseph Bonyata, director of publications, for his leadership, support, and encouragement; Shirley S. Ricks, senior editor, for her vision, editorial professionalism, and attentiveness to details; Alicia M. Hill, accounting assistant, for her expertise (and enthusiasm) in locating and acquiring the images that appear in this book; Justin Kelly, book designer and typesetter, for his imagination and creativity in laying out the book's pages; and Caroline B. Larsen, intern, for her assistance in copyediting and proofreading.

The Greatest Archaeological Discovery

of the 20th Century

Texts versus Monuments

The Dead Sea Scrolls are astounding and spectacular discoveries. According to many scholars, the scrolls represent the greatest archaeological discovery of the twentieth century. The scrolls stand with other notable archaeological discoveries of the same century, including Abu Simbel (two massive rock-cut temples in Egypt), Machu Picchu (fortified Inca town in the Andes Mountains, Peru), tomb of King Tutankhamun (Egyptian pharaoh of the Eighteenth Dynasty), Pompeii (buried by an eruption of Mount Vesuvius, Italy), Terracotta Army (Xi'an, China), Petra (temples and tombs hewn in cliffs in Jordan), and the (controversial) James ossuary.

The chief difference between the scrolls and other archaeological discoveries, however, is that the scrolls consist of texts rather than being monuments or nontextual artifacts. The scrolls comprise an ancient library of more than 900 texts discovered between 1947 and 1956 in eleven caves near the northwest shore of the Dead Sea; hence the collection is named the Dead Sea Scrolls. About 225 of the scrolls contain texts from the Old Testament, and most of the remaining scrolls are nonbiblical religious texts.

The Terracotta Army (Xi'an, China) consists of sculptures of armies of Qin Shi Huang (China's first emperor); the sculptures were buried with the emperor around 209 BC. Image depicts a close-up of one of the soldiers.

Mask of Tutankhamun (Egyptian pharaoh of the Eighteenth Dynasty). Tutankhamun's tomb contained an abundance of rich contents.

Petra, an ancient Nabataean city (now in present-day Jordan), features prominent tombs and temples that were hewn from red sandstone cliffs. The photo depicts Al Khazneh (the treasury).

An Astonishing Discovery: The First Seven Scrolls

The fact that the Dead Sea Scrolls had remained undiscovered in caves for about two millennia is indeed a miracle. How could the scrolls have escaped notice throughout the centuries when pilgrims, travelers, and others sought temporary lodging in caves throughout the region? And what about individuals and families who inhabited caves on a long-term basis? How could they not have noticed the jars, scrolls, or scroll fragments in those caves of Qumran? Remarkably, the scrolls remained undiscovered for centuries, and yet ultimately they were brought to light.

Some of the facts regarding the discovery of the Dead Sea Scrolls are elusive or contradictory, in part because those who participated in the discovery relied on their memories as they recounted the events. The basic facts follow: Early in 1947 (or, according to another account, late in 1946), three shepherds belonging to the Ta'amireh Bedouin—Muhammed edh-Dhib (Muhammed Ahmed el-Hamed), Jum'a Muhammed Khalil, and Khalil Musa—discovered scrolls in what is now called Qumran Cave 1. Perhaps the three were playing a game to see who could hit the cave opening with a rock, or maybe they were searching for a stray goat or sheep. In any case, one of them cast a rock into a cave opening, which resulted

Bedouin shepherds discovered several scrolls in Qumran Cave 1, which is located in the face of a rock cliff.

in the breaking of an earthen jar. They were frightened off by the sound. Possibly the next day, edh-Dhib and perhaps one or two others returned to the site and climbed into the cave. He/they discovered several large clay jars, perhaps as many as ten and maybe more. Many of the jars had lids, some of which were sealed to the jars. After removing the lids, the Bedouin discovered several scrolls in a remarkable state of preservation. In the course of time, the Bedouin discovered seven scrolls in

Accessing impossible places

"Just how the bedouin succeeded in exiting the cave with their discoveries is also a relevant question, since the cave is described as virtually inaccessible (80 meters down from the top of an almost sheer cliff face)."

The greatest manuscript discovery of modern times

"In my excitement, I began writing on the wrong side of the sheet! I repeat that in my opinion you have made the greatest MS discovery of modern times—certainly the greatest biblical MS find."

Trever, *The Untold Story*, 85, quoting a letter from William F. Albright to John Trever, arrived March 15, 1948, in DJD XXXII, 10.

this cave—the Habakkuk Commentary, the Rule of the Community, the Genesis Apocryphon, the Great Isaiah Scroll, a second Isaiah scroll, the Thanksgiving Hymns, and the War Scroll.

For a period of time the Bedouin did not realize the significance of their finds. During the ensuing weeks the Bedouin stored some of the scrolls in a bag on a tent pole. As they showed them to others, small pieces of leather fell off. Reportedly, children played with one scroll and destroyed it. If this were the case, we may never know the contents of that scroll. The Bedouin deemed the scrolls' cloth wrappings and the scroll fragments to be worthless and so threw them aside (such fragments now sell for millions of dollars). The Bedouin used two jars from Cave 1 as water jars in their camp. According to one early account, the Bedouin carried one or more scrolls to Bethlehem, hoping that a shoemaker would make sandals out of one of the leather scrolls.

Muhammad edh-Dhib, one of the shepherds who discovered the Dead Sea Scrolls, holds a lamb (note Bedouin tents in the background).

The Bedouin were not alone in failing to recognize the scrolls' significance. In the early months after the discovery of the scrolls, antiquities dealers, scholars, and ecclesiastics also incorrectly assessed their value. In order to ascertain the scrolls' worth, various individuals examined one or more of the scrolls but incorrectly assessed their date, provenance, or value. For example, Bethlehem antiquities dealers Ibrahim 'Ijha and Faidi Salahi saw one or more of the scrolls. 'Ijha claimed the scrolls had "no archaeological value," and Salahi supposed that the Bedouin had stolen them from a synagogue. Also, Old Testament scholar J. P. M. van der Ploeg (University of Nijmegen) was conducting research at the École Biblique in Jerusalem in 1947. Sometime in July of that year, he examined the Great Isaiah Scroll and incorrectly determined that it was a medieval manuscript.

Declaring the scrolls to have no archaeological value

"In Bethlehem in February or March 1947, Khalil and Jum'a showed their three scrolls (1QIsa[a], 1QpHab, and 1QS) to Ibrahim 'Ijha, a carpenter and antiquities dealer. He in turn took them to Faidi Salahi, another antiquities dealer, who suspected they had been stolen from a synagogue. After several weeks (around 5 April 1947) Ibrahim returned the manuscripts to Jum'a, declaring them to be of no archaeological value."

DJD XXXII, 3.

The scrolls of Cave 1 were stored in large terracotta jars. This storage system preserved several scrolls for more than 2,000 years.

Metropolitan Samuel in the center, flanked by Father Butrus Sowmy on the left with the Commentary on Habakkuk, and John Trever on the right with the Great Isaiah Scroll.

Other individuals inaccurately evaluated the scrolls' provenance or age. When scholar Toviah Wechsler from Jerusalem examined the Great Isaiah Scroll, he concluded that it (and the other scrolls) had been stolen from a synagogue (a conclusion also held by Salahi; see above). George Isha'ya Shamoun, a businessman from Bethlehem, thought the language of the scrolls was Syriac, suggesting he believed that the scrolls were of Christian origin. Two librarians from the Hebrew University viewed one or more of the scrolls and thought they were of Samaritan origin, and the Syrian Patriarch in Homs, Syria, considered them as recent as the last three centuries.

During the ensuing weeks, John Trever became a major player in the unfolding story of the scrolls. Trever was an American biblical scholar who was in Jerusalem at the time as a visiting fellow at the American School of Oriental Research (ASOR, a research center for ancient Near Eastern studies located in Jerusalem). On February 18, 1948, Father Butrus Sowmy from St. Mark's Monastery telephoned ASOR with the intent of speaking to a scholar concerning the age of the scrolls. Trever, who was in the right place at the right time, took the call. Sowmy and Trever met the following day. Trever recounted seeing the Great Isaiah Scroll for the first time:

> They lifted from the satchel a large scroll, about 10" long and 6" in diameter, and handed it to me. Removing the Arabic newspaper, I saw that this scroll was made of thinner, softer leather and was much more pliable. It was about the same color as the first one, but with a darkened center, evidence of much handling. It unrolled easily.
>
> Laying the heavy document on my bed, slowly I began to open it. A sheet of leather, containing two columns of text, had become detached from the rest of the document. The linen thread used to bind the sheets together had disintegrated. On the

Jum'a Muhammed Khalil and Muhammed edh-Dhib, in the middle of this photograph, were instrumental in discovering the Cave 1 scrolls; Anton Kiraz, a businessman who assisted Metropolitan Samuel is on the left, and J.F. Docmac is on the right.

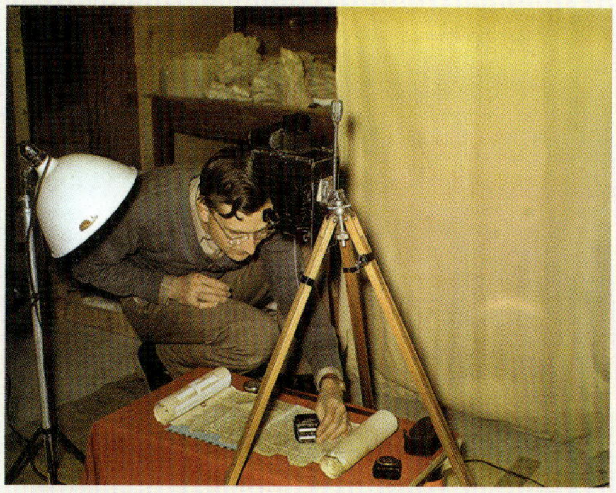

In February and March 1948, John Trever photographed a few Cave 1 scrolls in the basement of the American School of Oriental Research in Jerusalem. Trever, the first person ever to photograph the scrolls, has made significant contributions to Dead Sea Scrolls research.

> left edge the text was badly blurred by someone who had attempted to re-ink many letters which had been worn away by handling. Obviously this was the end of the scroll. It had been rolled backwards, with the last column on the outside. I continued to unroll another six to eight columns.[1]

Soon after Trever viewed this Isaiah scroll, he convinced his guests to allow him to photograph three of the scrolls—1QIsa[a], 1QpHab, and 1QS. In the basement of ASOR, Trever began his historic photographing efforts. His photographs, of excellent quality, are still widely used today, even though the camera equipment he used was of mid-nineteenth-century vintage. Also during the course of the day, Trever spent some time repairing and patching tiny fragments that had fallen from the Isaiah scroll during handling. Lacking a professional, museum-quality adhesive, Trever used common scotch tape to bond the fragments to the scroll:

> Scotch tape was all we had to use, but I carefully applied it to the back of the breaks to avoid any possible damage to the script. Setting the various pieces in their proper places was like working a huge jigsaw puzzle. The Syrians stood close by, keenly watching every move. The Metropolitan leaned so close to my shoulder as I bent over the scroll that his beard tickled my neck. I dared not complain! With each successful placement, he uttered an ejaculation of delight.[2]

After developing photographs of the Isaiah scroll, Trever sent a letter and sample photographs to American scholar William F. Albright. The letter explained:

> Enclosed are some sample prints from a manuscript. . . . If you are right about your dating of the Nash Papyrus, then I believe that this is the oldest Biblical document yet discovered! . . . I firmly believe the script cannot be later than the 2nd Cent.

Taking pictures of the scrolls

"Inscribed fragments were mounted between glass each day as they were found, and photographed on the spot for safe record. Infra-red photographs taken in the studio of the Palestine Archaeological Museum later have revealed texts on pieces which to the naked eye present merely a blank black surface."

G. Lankester Harding, "Introductory," in DJD I, 7.

> A.D. (Dura Fragment), and it has some indications to show it may be earlier than the Nash Papyrus. I am so busy with the photographing of them that I can't take time now to make the careful study that they demand for more accurate dating. I am personally convinced that their age is great. . . . I know you will understand my concern about the safety of the MSS, so will keep this absolutely confidential. Should there be an announcement now, there is great danger that they might be destroyed.[3]

On March 15, a little more than two weeks later, Trever received a dramatic response from Albright, who relayed that his "eyes bulged when [he] saw the script" of the Isaiah scroll. Albright also exclaimed, "What an absolutely incredible find!"

John Trever and Metropolitan Samuel examine the Great Isaiah Scroll. Note two other scrolls on the desk.

> Dear Trever,
>
> Your air-letter of Feb. 25th, with its enclosures, arrived this morning and I immediately got out my magnifying glass and started in. I am now having the prints enlarged so I can study the script to better advantage. My heartiest congratulations on the greatest MS [manuscript] discovery of modern times! There is no doubt whatever in my mind that the script is more archaic than that of the Nash Papyrus, . . . I should prefer a date around 100 B.C. The script is in every respect older than that of the Dura parchment fragment.
>
> In my excitement I began writing on the wrong side of the sheet! I repeat that in my opinion you have made the greatest MS discovery of modern times—certainly the greatest biblical MS find. The spelling is most interesting . . . Let us hope that nothing happens to your precious finds!
>
> I don't anticipate any very significant textual corrections of the text of Isaiah, but the new material will revolutionize our conception of the development of Hebrew orthography. And who knows what treasures may be concealed in the remaining rolls!
>
> It is a very fine thing that you have been able to get such an important result as this discovery from your difficult year in Jerusalem. You can imagine how my eyes bulged when I saw the script through my magnifying glass! What an absolutely incredible find! And there can happily not be the slightest doubt in the world about the genuineness of the MS.
>
> Cordially,
> W. F. Albright[4]

"I spent several hours at the underground Jerusalem Haganah Headquarters, toured the city with the Haganah commander, and just before returning to Tel-Aviv I went to visit my parents. My father, Elazar L. Sukenik, was the Professor of Archaeology at the Hebrew University. I found him in a state of high exhilaration, eyes glowing with excitement. 'What shall I do?' he asked me after our exchange of *shaloms*. 'Shall I go to Bethlehem? I must. First thing in the morning. What do you say?' I gathered that he had made an exciting archaeological discovery but I could not guess what it was."

Yigael Yadin, *The Message of the Scrolls* (New York: Crossroad, 1992), 15–16.

Finally the scroll's antiquity and academic value were authenticated. In time, this and the other scrolls would be designated the greatest archaeological discovery of the twentieth century.

Word of the authentication traveled quickly in academic and other circles. On April 12, 1948, the *Times* newspaper of London released the first report to an international audience:

> Yale University announced yesterday the discovery in Palestine of the earliest known manuscript of the Book of Isaiah. It was found in the Syrian monastery of St. Mark in Jerusalem, where it had been preserved in a scroll of parchment dating to about the first century BC. Recently it was identified by scholars of the American School of Oriental Research at Jerusalem.
>
> There were also examined at the school three other ancient Hebrew scrolls. One was part of a commentary on the Book of Habakkuk; another seemed to be a manual of discipline of some comparatively little-known sect or monastic order, possibly the Essenes. The third scroll has not yet been identified.

Although the newspaper report contained factual errors, the world had thus received news of the scrolls' discovery.

A Gold Mine of Texts

Those who discovered the texts of Qumran truly struck gold. How so? Because they discovered a broad assortment of invaluable texts, including portions of the world's oldest Hebrew Bible, poetic compositions and Wisdom literature, biblical commentaries, writings used during worship, business records, texts used during prayer, calendrical texts, legal documents, a record detailing the whereabouts of hidden treasures, plus others. Altogether, these various texts make the Dead Sea Scrolls exceptionally significant, better than baskets of precious jewels and barrels of pearls.

The Qumran scrolls belong to a variety of categories and types of texts; some texts, such as the Temple Scroll, belong to two different categories. The categories of the scrolls include:

Books of the Hebrew Bible

Except for Esther, every book of the Hebrew Bible—including Genesis, Exodus, 1 and 2 Samuel, Isaiah, and Malachi—was represented in the Qumran caves.

Parabiblical texts
Literature that is Bible-like, or "closely related to texts or themes of the Hebrew Bible,"[5] include the Temple Scroll, Epistle of Jeremiah, Book of Enoch, Book of Noah, Genesis Apocryphon, Jubilees, Testament of Levi, Text Mentioning the Flood, Testament of Judah, Apocryphon of Moses, Visions of Amram, Text concerning Rachel, Testament of Joseph, Apocryphon of Joshua, Prophecy of Joshua, New Jerusalem, Apocryphon of Jeremiah, Prayer of Enosh, Apocryphon of Levi, and others. These religious writings present particulars that increase our understanding of many elements of history, culture, and religious thought.

Aramaic translations of the Hebrew Bible
These translations were intended for Aramaic speakers and include portions of the books of Job, Leviticus, and others.

Exegetical texts
Exegesis is the interpretation or explanation of a text. Qumran yielded different types of exegetical texts, including commentaries (Hebrew *pesharim*) of Isaiah, Hosea, Micah, Nahum, Zephaniah, Malachi, and Psalms; as well as a list of false prophets found in the Old Testament (4QList of False Prophets), a brief listing of messianic prophecies (4QTestimonia), and other exegetical texts.

The Book of Mysteries, discovered in Cave 1, belongs to the category of Wisdom literature.

A magical text written on papyrus from Wadi Murabba'at; note the figure of a man on the right side of the fragment.

Historical texts and tales

This classification includes Tobit, Historical Texts, and Proto-Esther.

Writings for worship

These texts pertain to the worship practices of the Qumran people and provide particulars regarding prayers, blessings, hymns, and rituals. The writings include Benedictions; Bless, My Soul; Purification Ritual; Prayer or Hymn Celebrating the Morning and the Evening; the Thanksgiving Hymns; Daily Prayers; Blessings; and Prayers for Festivals.

Texts concerned with religious law

Religious legal texts that describe rules and regulations belonging to the Qumran community include the Damascus Document, the Rule of the Community, the Rule of the Congregation, Some Observances of the Law, plus others.

Tefillin and mezuzot

Approximately thirty *tefillin* (singular, *tefillah*), also called phylacteries (see Matthew 23:5), and *mezuzot* (singular, *mezuzah*) comprise this category.

Why were the scrolls hidden in caves?

"The reason for their being thus secreted in caves appears to be that the settlement at Qumrân, of whose library they formed a part, was being threatened with attack, probably by the Romans who were engaged in suppressing the first Jewish Revolt."

G. Lankester Harding, "Introductory," in DJD I, 4.

Writings that focus on the last days
Religious texts describing events that would supposedly occur at the end of time include the Words of Michael, New Jerusalem, Apocryphon of Daniel, Four Kingdoms, Vision, Renewed Earth, Messianic Apocalypse, Eschatological Hymn, and others.

Poetic and liturgical texts
This classification includes the Ritual of Marriage, Liturgical Work, Purification Liturgy, the Thanksgiving Hymns, Laments, Hymns, Eschatological Hymn, plus others.

Wisdom literature
Many poems pertain to the study and obtaining of wisdom, including Instruction, Mysteries, the Two Ways, The Seductress, Admonitory Parable, Beatitudes, and Meditation on Creation.

Calendrical texts
Writings that deal with the calendar and festivals include Calendric Signs, Calendars of Priestly Courses, Calendrical Document, Zodiacal Calendar, Horoscopes, Lunisolar Calendar, Daily Prayers, Prayers for Festivals, and others.

Documentary texts
These types of scrolls contain business records noting accounts of money and grain, the sale of property, records pertaining to debt, deeds of sale, deeds of slave sales, loans, promissory notes, marriage contracts, and more.

Treasure list
The Copper Scroll is a fascinating record of treasures that were hidden in various locations throughout ancient Palestine.

Magic and divination
These types of scrolls include curses, incantation, exorcism, and others.[6]

Eleven Extraordinary Caves

Of the hundreds of caves located in the Holy Land, eleven are extraordinary because they sheltered the Dead Sea Scrolls for about 2,000 years. For convenience, scholars call these caves, in order of their discovery, Qumran Cave 1, Qumran Cave 2, and so on. The Ta'amireh tribesmen discovered the scrolls of Caves 1, 2, 4, 6, and 11; archaeologists or workmen were responsible for finding the scrolls of Caves 3, 5, and 7–10.

Some of the Cave 1 scrolls were found intact, carefully wrapped in linen and stored in jars, indicating that an individual or individuals had time to carefully prepare the scrolls for storage. The difficult access to the cave seems to indicate that it was used chiefly as a hiding place for the scrolls. The scrolls found in the other caves seem to have been placed there hastily without protection against the elements; hence most scrolls now exist only

Map of Dead Sea showing nearby caves in relation to Qumran.

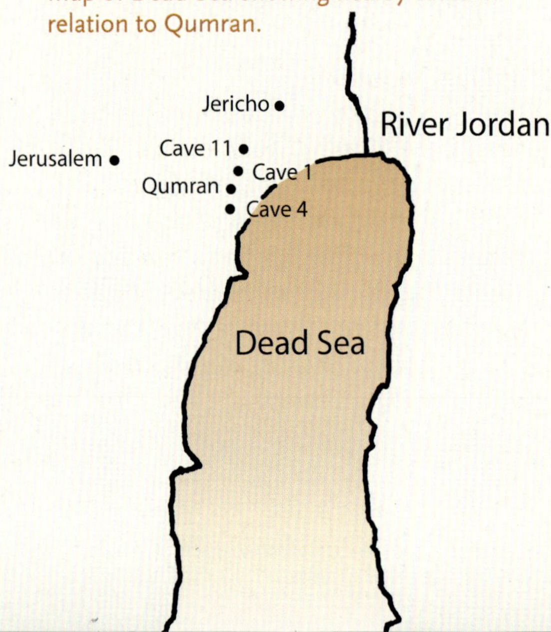

in a fragmentary condition. Cave 1 yielded seven major scrolls: the Great Isaiah Scroll, a second Isaiah scroll, Rule of the Community, the War Scroll, the Thanksgiving Hymns, the Genesis Apocryphon, and the Habakkuk Commentary.

Cave 3 contained the Copper Scroll, a twelve-column text that describes the location of enormous, presumed treasures.

Cave 4, which seems to be a man-made cave, yielded the largest cache of scrolls—hundreds of manuscripts and thousands of fragments. Cave 4 yielded dozens of biblical texts, including eighteen (fragmented) copies of Isaiah. Archaeologists surmise that the scrolls of Cave 4 were once stored on wooden shelves that no longer exist. Unfortunately, for centuries the scrolls were exposed to the elements on the cave floor.

Cave 11 yielded the famous Temple Scroll (the longest of the Dead Sea Scrolls), the Psalms Scroll, and many fragmented texts.

In addition to the eleven Qumran caves, searchers discovered additional texts in other locations in the Judaean Desert to the west of the Dead Sea—Wadi Murabba'at, Masada, Naḥal Hever, Naḥal Ṣe'elim, Khirbet Mird, Naḥal Mishmar, and Wadi Daliyeh. These texts are also sometimes categorized as Dead Sea Scrolls.

Ancient Ruins of Qumran

Qumran is the Arabic name for the stone ruins located on a high plateau near the northwestern shore of the Dead Sea. The ruins encompass a small area, about an acre. The eleven caves that yielded the Dead Sea Scrolls are near the Qumran ruins. Some of the caves are located along cliffs on the southern edge of Qumran, while others are found about a kilometer north of Qumran. Unfortunately,

Located close to the Qumran ruins, Cave 4 yielded more scrolls and scroll fragments than all other caves combined.

Interior of Cave 4, where hundreds of scrolls were discovered.

Qumran Cave 11 yielded the famous Temple Scroll, the longest of the scrolls, and the Psalms Scroll, a magnificent example of a manuscript that belonged to the world of antiquity.

View of the Dead Sea from Masada, which is located on its southwestern shore.

scholars have reached no consensus about who occupied Qumran. Although varying theories concerning the occupants of Qumran exist, scholars have presented arguments against most of these theories.

Qumran served as a countryside villa

Major arguments against this theory mention the barrenness of the area, the salty soil, the harsh climate, and the lack of a constant water source. Furthermore, the archaeological remains exhibit no elaborate architectural components, mosaic floors, painted walls, fancy bathhouses, and structures associated with beautiful gardens. In short, this area is an undesirable location for a villa and is unlike other areas in the country where villas were present.

Aerial view of the Qumran ruins with the Dead Sea in the background.

Qumran served as a fortress

Before Roland de Vaux excavated the site in the 1950s, the prevailing view was that Qumran had been an old fortress, perhaps of Roman origin. Challenges to this theory involve the lack of evidence for compound walls or other elements that denote a fortification; also, the study of the ruins suggests that the entrances to the complex were unguarded. In sum, Qumran was unlike other fortresses in the greater region.

Qumran was a fortified estate in the country

To a certain extent, this theory combines the first two suggestions. Again, the area lacks arable land and a consistent water source, and the elements are too harsh and dry to consider Qumran to be a country estate.

Qumran served as a commercial center

Qumran is less accessible, geographically speaking, than other known commercial centers in the greater region; additionally, Qumran did not exist on a major trade route, making the commercial center theory unlikely.

Qumran served as a community center of a Jewish sect

For a handful of reasons, this is the most widely accepted theory today (although some scholars challenge this assumption, too). The following points provide evidence supporting this theory:

Ritual immersion pools. Of the sixteen water installations located at Qumran, six serve as cisterns and the other ten are thought to be ritual immersion pools. Ritual pools are distinguished from cisterns because stairs lead down to the pools; also, demarcation features or indicators located on

Ruins of Qumran. Many scholars maintain that a Jewish sect resided near here.

the stairs usually serve to separate ritually unclean persons (those descending to the pool) from ritually clean persons (those ascending from the pool). These ritual immersion pools help to identify Qumran as a religious compound of some sort.

Large kitchen/dining hall/pantry. Archaeologists identified a kitchen with a number of fireplaces that served as cooking ovens, a dining hall designed to accommodate 100–150 persons, and a nearby pantry that contained about 1,000 pottery vessels. The dining hall may have had a double purpose, also serving as an assembly hall for religious meetings.

Scriptorium. The excavator Roland de Vaux identified one of the rooms at Qumran as a scriptorium, a room where scribes copied manuscripts. He based his classification on two factors: (1) three inkwells were discovered in the immediate area, suggesting that scribal activities were carried out; and (2) three table-like structures were also discovered in the area. These structures were made of a mixture of rubble and mud, which was then covered with mortar and plaster. The shape of these structures is unusual: about 16 feet long, 1.6 feet wide, and 2.3 feet high. These structures did not have table legs, as one in the modern world would expect; rather, the structures' support system consisted of solid material that diminished in width as it reached the floor. Scholars have suggested varying purposes for these structures—for example, as benches, tables, or couches. Many scholars presume that scribes used the structures as special work surfaces to copy the manuscripts.

Potter's workshop. Archaeologists located and identified a potter's workshop at

According to many scholars, this large room at Qumran was a scriptorium, where scribes made new copies of scriptures and other writings.

Qumran with two kilns, a pit to store the clay, and a potter's wheel. A potter's workshop of this size was normally unnecessary for a small community, but perhaps this workshop served a special purpose. In order to keep their vessels pure, the Jewish sect may have needed a constant supply of new vessels. The Qumran community could also have supplied vessels to other communities.

Animal bones. Workers uncovered carefully buried animal bones, a possible indication that the bones were the remains of sacrificial offerings. But the idea of Jews offering animal sacrifices outside the Jerusalem temple (at this time) is improbable. Another possible explanation for the buried bones is that they were the remains of sacred meals.

According to many scholars, the inhabitants of Qumran probably did not dwell in the complex of buildings but resided in nearby caves, as evidenced by the more than two dozen caves showing signs of occupation. Many of these residential caves have leveled floors, some form of ventilation, and natural light and are roomy enough for inhabitants. Furthermore, archaeological finds include potsherds, jars, utensils, tableware, coins, and personal items such as combs or textile remains.

The size of the cemetery located near the ruins and other archaeological evidence indicate that the community founded at Qumran may have numbered about 200 individuals at any one time. The building complex at Qumran appears to have originally been occupied about 140 BC, while the final destruction dates to about AD 68. When the community first came to Qumran, it was much smaller

Three table-like structures (now on display at the Rockefeller Museum) were discovered in the scriptorium of Qumran. Perhaps scribes copied scriptures on these structures.

in size. However, some decades later the building complex was enlarged, and the community continued to grow until 31 BC. The historian Josephus reports a large earthquake in Palestine at that time, and archaeological evidence confirms that an earthquake and fire caused the first destruction of the community. The area was eventually reoccupied, at the latest probably around 4 BC.

The stairs leading down to a ritual pool at Qumran were split by an earthquake about 31 BC.

A large cistern at Qumran that provided water to local inhabitants.

The Dead Sea Scrolls—Superstar among Ancient Text Discoveries

Both archaeological discoveries and accidental finds have uncovered a large number of texts from a variety of locations in the Holy Land and neighboring countries. Over the past recent decades numerous discoveries of ancient texts have come to light. These include the Ebla tablets, Gilgamesh Epic, Enuma Elish, Nuzi tablets, Code of Hammurabi, Mari tablets, Ras Shamra tablets, Amarna letters, Wisdom of Amenemope, Gezer Calendar, Mesha Stele, Sargon II's inscription, Lachish letters, Cyrus Cylinder, and Elephantine papyri. The earliest of these texts dates to the third millennium BC, and the latest to the last decades before the destruction of the Jerusalem temple in AD 70. The manuscripts are written in various languages—Sumerian, Eblaite, Ugaritic, Akkadian, Egyptian, Moabite, Aramaic, and Hebrew.

When taken together, these manuscripts or texts number in the thousands. The Ebla texts by themselves comprise an archive of about 18,000 texts; the Mari clay tablets number approximately 22,000; and the Dead Sea Scrolls include about 900 compositions (though most are fragmented).

These different text discoveries consist of a variety of literary and documentary types, including biblical, parabiblical, apocryphal, pseudepigraphic, and other religious texts; they also consist of Wisdom literature, letters, legal contracts and documents, chronicles, food lists, tax or tribute lists, an engineering document, commercial documents, kings' reigns lists, brief histories, poetry, epic literature, and accounts of military sieges, conquests, and victories. Collectively, the texts provide historical, socioreligious, political, and commercial information that sheds light on most historical periods of the Old Testament.

Of all these textual discoveries, one group is by far more popular than the rest—the Dead Sea Scrolls. More than other ancient text discoveries, the scrolls are spotlighted at museum exhibits around the world, discussed at academic conferences, and examined in literally thousands of books, articles, theses, or dissertations. Furthermore, dictionaries and encyclopedias are dedicated to bringing the scrolls to light, the popular press produces information regarding them, and nonacademic audiences investigate their contents.

So, why are the scrolls of such academic value? The answer lies in what we learn from them and what topics they cover:

- Old Testament studies, including the history and transmission of the biblical text and variant readings in the text
- scribal schools and their practices and methodologies
- Hebrew and Aramaic linguistic studies
- apocryphal and pseudepigraphic studies
- the study of religious groups and their ideas within Palestinian Judaism
- ancient methods of biblical interpretation
- the history of Jewish groups between the years 250 BC and AD 70
- background studies for the rise of Christianity

And this is just the beginning.

Incrustations, dirt, and decay—cleaning scroll fragments

"On arrival at the Palestine Museum, purchased groups of fragments were in unbelievable disorder. Many large, well-preserved fragments came in each lot. But large or small, well or ill preserved, most had to be exposed to a process of humidification, cleaned of incrustations and dirt, and repaired or reinforced before being pressed flat between glass plates. Fragments in advanced decay, especially lumps of coagulated layers of leather, require more energy and patience and special techniques, though the same general procedure is followed."

Frank Moore Cross, *The Ancient Library of Qumran*, 3rd ed. (Minneapolis, MN: Fortress Press, 1995), 39–40.

Writing Materials—Skins, Papyrus, Copper, and Ostraca

The great majority of the scrolls are written on animal skins. The skins had to be from clean animals as defined by the law of Moses (see Leviticus 11:3–8 and Deuteronomy 14:4–8); this included sheep, gazelle, ibex, and deer. Moreover, the quill pen, ink, and threads that attached the leather sheets together had to be formally prepared in conformance with the Mosaic code. Other scrolls are written on papyrus, which is made from the stems of a water plant. One scroll inscribed on copper sets forth the whereabouts of hidden treasures. And several ostraca (singular, *ostracon*), or potsherds, have writings on them.

Purchasing three scrolls for $20

"Eventually, the three scrolls were brought to Khalil Eskander Shahin, better known as Kando, another antiquities dealer who had a shop near Nativity Square in Bethlehem. Kando agreed to pay five Jordanian pounds (roughly equivalent to fourteen British pounds or twenty U.S. dollars at the time) to the Bedouin."

DJD XXXII, 3.

Selling and Reselling the Scrolls for Profit

Once it was determined that the scrolls and fragments were of great worth, many were purchased and then resold at higher prices. Antiquities dealers, collectors, museums, and universities played various roles in the acquisition of the scrolls. Some transactions were for profit, others resulted in the acquisition of scrolls for academic study and publication.

The story of the selling and reselling of four of the scrolls—the Great Isaiah Scroll, the Habakkuk Commentary, the Rule of the Community, and the Genesis Apocryphon—contains both intrigue and interest. In March 1947 (or perhaps earlier), Khalil and Jum'a went to Bethlehem with the intent of selling the scrolls. They presented the scrolls to Ibrahim 'Ijha, an antiquities dealer, who then showed them to Faidi Salahi, another dealer. Salahi believed the scrolls to be stolen. Soon thereafter, perhaps in April 1947, Jum'a showed the scrolls to a third dealer of antiquities, also from Bethlehem. His name was Khalil Eskander Shahin, better known as Kando. After inspecting the scrolls, Kando agreed to purchase the scrolls for five Jordanian pounds (about $20).

Kando, an antiquities dealer from Bethlehem, had an important role in the purchase of scrolls from Cave 1.

Cheating someone for scroll fragments

"Abu Daoud claimed that the antiquities dealer Kando 'cheated him out of some fragments, so he tried to kill Kando with a knife, and that Kando had the scar on his neck to prove it.'"

Weston W. Fields, *The Dead Sea Scrolls: A Full History* (Leiden: Brill, 2009), 1:153.

Kando immediately sought a buyer for the scrolls. By mid-April 1947, the Metropolitan (the title of a ranking bishop) Athanasius Yeshue Samuel at St. Mark's Syrian Orthodox Monastery in Jerusalem agreed to purchase all four scrolls. On July 19, 1947, he purchased them for 24 Jordanian pounds (about $96). These four scrolls became known as the "St. Mark's Monastery Scrolls." Before the Metropolitan actively sought a buyer for the scrolls, he approached experts to determine the scrolls' value. Later, after scholars had established the antiquity and archaeological value of the scrolls, the Metropolitan set their price at $1,000,000.

In December 1948 or January 1949, the Metropolitan traveled to the United States, in part to fulfill a new ecclesiastical appointment, Apostolic Delegate of the Syrian Church. The Metropolitan carried with him the four scrolls. Upon arriving in the state of New Jersey, he again tried to sell them. Meanwhile, the scrolls were exhibited at the Library of Congress in Washington (October 1949) and later at Duke University and the University of Chicago (sometime during 1950). But not only was the selling price of the scrolls too high ($1,000,000), but there remained questions regarding the Metropolitan's legal right to own and sell the scrolls. After four years, the Metropolitan then took an unconventional approach to selling the scrolls by placing an advertisement in the classified section of the *Wall Street Journal*. On June 1, 1954, under the heading MISCELLANEOUS FOR SALE, the following advertisement appeared:

MISCELLANEOUS FOR SALE

"The Four Dead Sea Scrolls"

Biblical Manuscripts dating back to at least 200 BC, are for sale. This would be an ideal gift to an educational or religious institution by an individual or group.

Box F 206, The Wall Street Journal.

The *Wall Street Journal* advertises four Dead Sea Scrolls for sale in a classified ad (June 1, 1954).

Metropolitan Samuel dressed in his Orthodox Christian sacred vestments.

An early attempt to purchase the scrolls

"It was Friday, 6 February that I made my way again to Zone B with the precious scrolls in my hand. I feared that I might never see them again. In the YMCA the Syrian [Kiraz] was waiting for me. Almost his first question was 'how much do you offer?' I countered by asking him to name the price. Neither of us would name the figure, and we finally arranged to meet the following week at the Yugoslav Consulate [where the guard was also a Syrian Christian]. He on his side would bring with him the metropolitan and I would bring with me Dr. Magnes, and we would try to reach agreement. I walked home slowly. The deserted streets fitted my mood of empty depression."

Weston W. Fields, *The Dead Sea Scrolls: A Full History* (Leiden: Brill, 2009) 1:53.

Through a series of events and small miracles, the four scrolls were purchased on June 15, 1954, for the sum of $250,000. Several months later the four scrolls were returned to Israel, for security reasons, in four different airplanes. On February 13, 1955, Premier Moshe Sharett made a significant announcement: the State of Israel had purchased the scrolls and would build a special museum to house them—the Shrine of the Book. After approximately 2,000 years, the scrolls were now back in the possession of a community of Hebrew speakers, a community with the ability to read the Dead Sea Scrolls.

Housing the Scrolls in Jerusalem

Most of the scrolls and fragments are presently housed in vaults in The Israel Museum, Jerusalem. The scrolls have been photographed and are stored under humidity- and temperature-controlled conditions. The seven major scrolls from Cave 1 are located in Jerusalem in the Shrine of the Book, which is part of the Israel Museum. The Shrine of the Book is unique because of its white, domed roof that resembles the shape of an earthenware lid similar to the lids that rested on the jars of Cave 1. Opposite this white dome stands a single, black basalt wall; the contrasting white and black symbolize the sons of light and the sons of darkness, who figure in the War Scroll.

The inside of the building is underground and resembles the interior of a cave. Displayed within this museum are numerous scrolls and scroll fragments, including a high-quality facsimile of the Great Isaiah Scroll. The Copper Scroll from Cave 3 and a number of fragments from Cave 1 are located at the Museum of the Department of Antiquities in Amman, Jordan. Additionally, investors or private parties in different places throughout the world own a number of scroll fragments.

The Shrine of the Book, which houses many Dead Sea Scrolls, has a roof designed to look like a Qumran jar lid. The color white symbolizes the sons of light.

Are there scrolls and fragments in private hands?

"It is possible that the additional portions of the scroll(s) fell into private hands and will some day surface. But for now, we must work with what we have, and it is severely fragmented and damaged."

Robert A. Craft, "Introduction: 6. Description of the Materials and Their State of Preservation," in DJD VIII, 16.

The interior of the Shrine of the Book features a large scroll handle.

The Bible and Biblical Studies

The Scrolls Feature the World's Oldest Old Testament

Of the approximately 900 scrolls and fragmented texts of the Dead Sea Scrolls, just over 200 represent books from the Old Testament,[1] including Genesis, Exodus, Leviticus, Joshua, Judges, Ruth, Isaiah, Jonah, and Daniel.[2] Multiple copies of a single work have also been found: Genesis (19–20 copies), Exodus (17), Leviticus (13), Numbers (7), Deuteronomy (30), Joshua (2), Judges (3), 1–2 Samuel (4), 1–2 Kings (3), Isaiah (21), Jeremiah (6), Ezekiel (6), Twelve Prophets (8–9),[3] Psalms (36), Proverbs (2), Job (4), Song of Solomon (4), Ruth (4), Lamentations (4), Ecclesiastes (2), Esther (0), Daniel (8), Ezra–Nehemiah (1), and 1–2 Chronicles (1).[4] The most popular books, based on the numbers alone, were Psalms, Deuteronomy, and Isaiah; the inhabitants of Qumran likely held these three scriptural books in great esteem. Likely not by coincidence, the early Christian community also held the same three Old Testament writings to be of great value, for they are the most frequently quoted scriptural books in the New Testament. The historical books (that is, Joshua, Judges, 1–2 Samuel, 1–2 Kings, and 1–2 Chronicles) were probably less important to the religious goals of the Jews who owned the scrolls.

With the exception of the book of Esther, at least fragments of every book of the Old Testament were discovered in the Qumran caves. One theory to account for the absence of the book of Esther is that perhaps fragments of the book did not survive the two millennia of decay

The Hebrew Bible (*left*) is opened to the book of Genesis.

The scroll of Deuteronomy from Cave 4 (columns 2–4) presents a very ancient copy of the Ten Commandments.

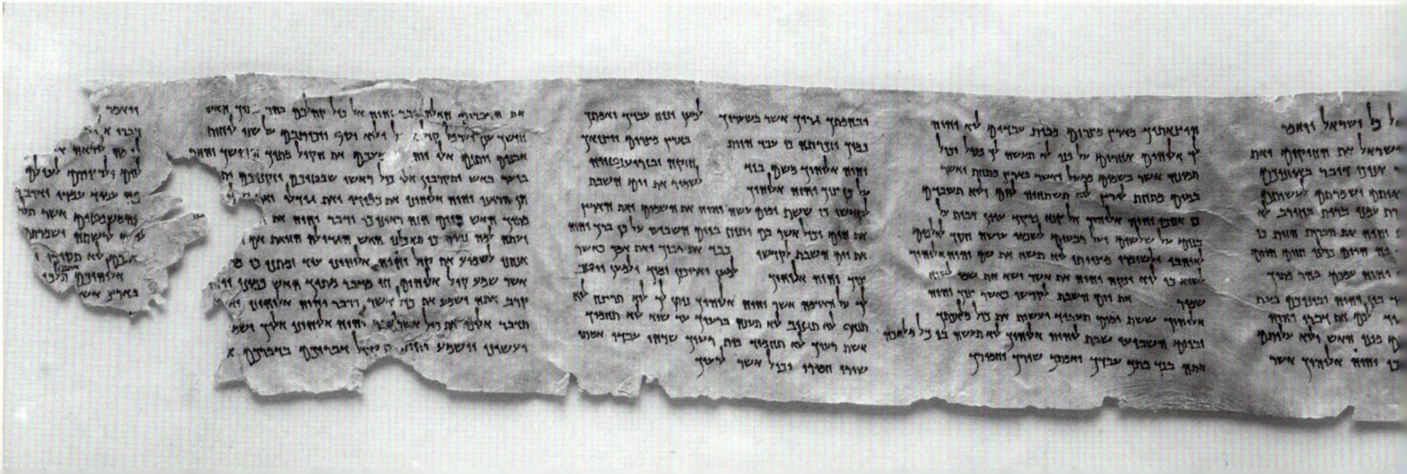

The Psalms Scroll from Cave 11 contains forty-nine hymns that were expressed on occasions of worship, reflection, and devotion.

in the caves. Other biblical books, such as 1–2 Chronicles and Ezra–Nehemiah, are highly fragmented; perhaps it is pure chance that we have these books and not Esther.

The biblical scrolls and fragments comprise texts that are 1,000 years older than the previously known texts of the Hebrew Bible. Most of the biblical texts of the Dead Sea Scrolls date from 150 BC to AD 68, although fragments from Exodus, Samuel, and Jeremiah have been dated to the middle of the third century BC. Consequently, these scrolls feature the world's oldest Hebrew Bible (that is, Christian Old Testament). Before the discovery of the scrolls, scholars relied on medieval manuscripts, often called the Masoretic Text (MT), for much of their understanding of the Old Testament. Three such manuscripts are the Leningrad Codex B 19a (complete Bible dated to AD 1009), the Cairo Codex of the Prophets (dated to AD 895), and the Aleppo Codex (dated to AD 925). These are considered late editions of the Hebrew Bible, especially since the ancient prophets such as Moses, Isaiah, and Amos wrote their books many centuries before the birth of Jesus Christ. We must keep in mind that biblical translators (for example, for the King James Version) accessed these medieval manuscripts, and *not* the much older Dead Sea Scrolls biblical manuscripts.

Why Are the Scrolls So Important to Biblical Studies?

The scrolls have been called the most important archaeological find of the twentieth century because of the way in which they have increased our knowledge of the Bible,

Second Temple Judaism (450 BC–AD 70), the Hebrew language, various religious texts, and much more. The scrolls have attracted so much attention that thousands of books, articles, dissertations, and other writings, as well as television documentaries and news stories, have focused on them. Also, new academic journals have appeared that are dedicated to the study of the scrolls, and professional conferences discuss their exceptional importance.

The scrolls significantly enhance scholarly research in many areas:

- The scrolls were discovered in the Holy Land, the land where Jesus and the ancient prophets and apostles lived.

- The scrolls are written in Hebrew, the language of the ancient prophets.

- The scrolls shed much light on the cultural, religious, and political position of some of the Jews who lived shortly before and during the time of Christ.

- The scrolls feature the world's oldest extant Hebrew Bible, which is more than 1,000 years older than the Masoretic Text (the Hebrew source of the King James Version and other bibles).

- Jewish scribes and copyists possessed a high level of competence as they transmitted the Bible from generation to generation; various scribal conventions disclose the nature of the scribal schools that produced the Dead Sea Scrolls.

Importance of the scrolls to the Bible

"Today, thanks to the marvellous literary windfall of the Qumran finds, our knowledge of the Hebrew Bible has been extended by another one thousand years or more (a Samuel manuscript from Cave 4 is said to date to about 225 BCE)."

Geza Vermes, *An Introduction to the Complete Dead Sea Scrolls* (Minneapolis, MN: Fortress Press, 1999), 172.

- The scrolls enlighten us concerning ancient scribal practices, including paragraphing, scribal corrections, and other various marks and notes in the text.
- The Dead Sea Scrolls Bible presents new readings that have been lost to our knowledge for about two millennia, including missing psalms and verses.
- Modern translation committees employ the Dead Sea Scrolls Bible as they prepare new translations of the Bible.
- The scrolls include the world's oldest complete book of Isaiah (23 feet 6 inches long).
- The scrolls include dozens of previously unknown religious texts, such as the Rule of the Community, the War Scroll, and the Temple Scroll.
- The Temple Scroll, the longest of the scrolls (about 28 feet long), is highly significant in part because it describes a future temple of Jerusalem.
- The Dead Sea Scrolls include dozens of parabiblical texts (texts that are Bible-like in character)—for example, the Book of Noah, Testament of Jacob, Testament of Judah, Apocryphon of Moses, Testament of Levi, Heavenly Prince Melchizedek, and Book of Enoch.
- The scrolls introduce and perhaps settle questions regarding which books belong(ed) to the scriptural canon of the Old Testament.
- The Copper Scroll details the whereabouts of massive hidden treasures of gold, silver, spices, and precious objects.
- The scrolls considerably increase our knowledge of the development of Hebrew and Aramaic.
- The scrolls disclose a great deal of information regarding archaic orthography (spelling practices), morphology (the form of words), and paleography (handwriting).
- The scrolls show us what the Bible looked like during the final decades that preceded Christianity; the scrolls also reveal the way the Old Testament was preserved, copied, and transmitted through the ages.
- The scrolls have been the focus of thousands of books, articles, monographs, dissertations, and other writings; academic journals are dedicated entirely to their study; and academic conferences discuss their significance.
- The scrolls are fascinating in their presentation of a number of puzzles and mysteries—for example, one scroll contains cryptic texts, other texts appear to be written in code, another is a mysterious text written backwards, another scroll features some words written in red ink rather than the standard black ink, and some scrolls depict the sacred name Jehovah with four dots.

- The scrolls disclose information regarding the manufacture of ancient scrolls from leather or papyrus, the linen thread that tied the pieces of parchment together, the consistency and quality of ink used for writing the scrolls, and more.

The Three Languages of Scripture

The biblical scrolls are written in three languages of ancient biblical scripture—Hebrew, Aramaic, and Greek. The language of about 90 percent of the scrolls is Hebrew, about 9 percent Aramaic, and less than 1 percent Greek. The majority of the scrolls, biblical and nonbiblical, were written in Hebrew, the language of the ancient prophets and the sacred language of the Jews. A few of the scrolls—including portions of the book of Daniel, the apocryphal book of Tobit, fragments of the books of Job and Leviticus, the Genesis Apocryphon, and the Book of Enoch—were written in Aramaic. Aramaic is a sister language to Hebrew, sharing with it the same alphabet and many grammatical features. A few Old Testament manuscripts were preserved in Greek.

Excursus: A Brief Lesson about Ancient Hebrew

Hebrew is a language that is read from right to left (backwards! Or is English backwards?). Ancient Hebrew (as it appears in the Dead Sea Scrolls) has consonants but no vowels. The scrolls were written without punctuation such as commas, periods, question marks, exclamation marks, or semicolons. Punctuation helps clarify the meaning of a clause or sentence, but since ancient Hebrew—including ancient

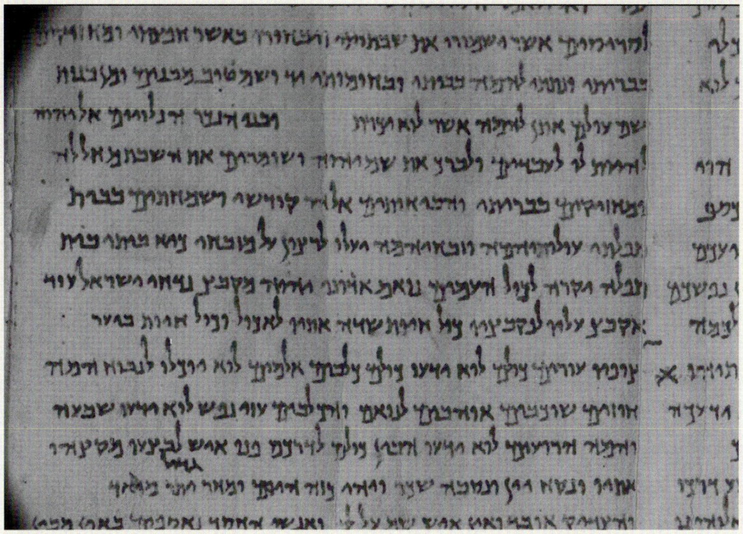

A portion of column 46 (=Isaiah 55:89–57:2) of the Great Isaiah Scroll, which was written in Hebrew. The book hand reveals that the scribe's writing was both skillful and polished.

Approximately 9 percent of the Dead Sea Scrolls are in Aramaic, including this book of Job from Cave 11.

Cave 7 yielded fragments of the book of Exodus written in Greek on papyrus.

biblical texts—lacked punctuation, that leaves the meanings of words and phrases open to interpretation. Hebrew does not have uppercase letters and, as is well known, is very different from English. Hebrew has a different font, syntax (sentence word order), morphology, grammar system, and accent system. The Hebrew language does not use the indefinite articles *a* and *an*, and it prefixes the definite article, some prepositions, and the conjunction *and* to a noun to make a single word, as in *andtheking* or *andtheprophet*. Further, the idea of chapters and verses was a later invention, although the scrolls do support evidence of an ancient paragraphing system. Consider the following, using English characters rather than Hebrew:

htrhtdn nvhht dtrc dg gnnngbhtn

Now read it backwards:

nthbgnnng gd crtd thhvn ndthrth

Now add the vowels:

inthebeginning god created theheaven andtheearth

Now separate the words:

in the beginning god created the heaven and the earth

And finally, use uppercase letters, add punctuation, and provide chapter and verse:

"In the beginning God created the heaven and the earth" (Genesis 1:1).

This provides a small glimpse into what students of Hebrew need to learn in order to read the Dead Sea Scrolls. Of course, the students have to learn to read Hebrew characters and to interpret various handwriting styles, not to mention to memorize an entirely new vocabulary.

What Did the Bible Look Like at the Time of Jesus Christ?

During his mortal ministry, Jesus Christ read from an Isaiah scroll in a synagogue in Nazareth (Luke 4:16–20). Although we do not know the appearance of this particular scroll, it was probably similar to the Great Isaiah Scroll discovered in Qumran Cave 1. As a matter of fact, the biblical Dead Sea Scrolls, collectively, provide us with a representation of what the Bible looked like at the time of Jesus and his disciples. The Bible Jesus read from likely had the following features:

- It was not a book with pages; rather, it consisted of a collection of individual scrolls, each independent of the other.
- The scrolls were made of leather parchment or papyri.
- Each scroll was unique as to the thickness, quality, and color of the leather, as well as the number of pieces of leather sewn together.
- Each scroll's columns, number of characters per line, and number of lines per column was also distinctive.
- The Bible at the time of Jesus had no chapters, verses, headers, or footnotes. (How did students of the Bible reference certain passages?)

- The handwriting on each scroll varied; each scribe who copied texts onto the leather possessed a unique handwriting style (the cursive, shape, and size of characters), just as each of us today has a singular approach to handwriting. Even students in the same elementary school with the same teacher have distinctive handwriting styles.

- Anciently, scribes regularly prepared scrolls for inscription by creating vertical and horizontal rulings to help them maintain orderly and straight lines for the characters. These rulings remind us of the ruled paper of modern times, but the scribes wrote on leather rather than on paper. These rulings justified the text on the top, bottom, and right margins (since Hebrew is read from right to left) and gave the composition a professional appearance that also made it easier to read. Incidentally, the scribes wrote the Hebrew letters under the line (hanging from the line) rather than on the line, as we do in English. The rulings were created with a writing instrument against a straight-edge utensil or, for dry-point rulings, scribes may have employed a sharp bone.

Modern Translations of the Bible Utilize the Dead Sea Scrolls Bible

Since the discovery of the scrolls, many contemporary translation committees of the Bible have paid special regard to the Dead Sea Scrolls biblical texts and have incorporated significant, new readings

Translation committees utilize both the Dead Sea Scrolls Bible and the Hebrew Bible (Masoretic Text) when they make new translations of the Bible. In the image below, the Masoretic Text stands next to the English translation of the Bible.

into their translations. According to Harold Scanlin, a translation adviser for the United Bible Societies, "every major Bible translation published since 1950 has claimed to have taken into account the textual evidence of the Dead Sea Scrolls."[5]

These readings are either incorporated into the actual translation of the Old Testament or are mentioned in footnotes or endnotes. The following English Bibles, for example, have integrated variant readings from the Dead Sea Scrolls Bible:

- New International Version
- Today's English Version
- Revised Standard Version
- New Revised Standard Version
- New English Bible
- New American Bible
- New King James Version
- Tanakh: The Holy Scriptures

Beyond these versions, many other translation committees have examined and subsequently integrated the variant readings of the Dead Sea Scrolls into their translations.

Here is an example of a reading that Tanakh: The Holy Scriptures (published by the Jewish Publication Society) has utilized in the book of Isaiah. In Isaiah 21:8, the Masoretic Text reads *lion*; the Great Isaiah Scroll (1QIsa[a]) reads *the watcher*, a word that better fits the context of the passage: "and the watcher cried, My lord, I stand continually upon the watchtower all day, and I am stationed at my post all night." Because *lion* and *the watcher* in the Hebrew language are graphically similar (*aryh* = *lion*; *hrah* = watcher), a copyist likely made a simple error when copying this word onto a new scroll that eventually became part of the Masoretic Text tradition.

Another example noted in Tanakh appears in Isaiah 33:8; here the Masoretic Text reads *cities* (*'rym*) versus the Great Isaiah Scroll's *witnesses* (*'dym*), again an example of graphic similarity in the Hebrew letters. The reading of the scroll corresponds well with the parallelism, "A covenant has been renounced, witnesses rejected."

"Arguing with myself" about the Great Isaiah Scroll

"Sleep was almost impossible that night. Numerous questions flooded my mind. How long was the large scroll? How much of Isaiah was there? Could it be authentic? Those few evidences of a corrector's hand on the last twelve columns seemed a certain argument for authenticity. But how could such a perfect manuscript be as old as the Nash Papyrus? Out of sheer exhaustion I fell asleep, still arguing with myself!"

The Great Isaiah Scroll, unrolled to reveal two columns of text, exemplifies a complete, beautiful scroll. This scroll is of great import to biblical studies.

A very recent translation of the Old Testament, entitled *The Dead Sea Scrolls Bible*, deserves special attention.[6] While the other English translations of the Bible (listed above) are chiefly based on the Masoretic Text and feature selections of variant readings from the scrolls, *The Dead Sea Scrolls Bible*, with some exceptions, presents a translation of the entire biblical corpus from the Dead Sea Scrolls. This makes *The Dead Sea Scrolls Bible* unique among modern translations of the Bible. *The Dead Sea Scrolls Bible* also includes other significant features, such as footnotes that compare readings from the Septuagint (Greek translation of the Bible) and the Masoretic Text.

Based on various scholars' positive reaction to the biblical scrolls, translation committees in future years will likely continue to accept variant readings from the biblical scrolls and fragments.

The Celebrated Great Isaiah Scroll (1QIsa[a])

Most of the scrolls are severely damaged and fragmented because of long-term exposure to the elements, but not so with the Great Isaiah Scroll (1QIsa[a]), which is perhaps the best-known scroll found at Qumran. This was one of the initial scrolls found in Qumran Cave 1 in 1947. Its preservation was enhanced because it was wrapped in a linen cloth and stored in a clay jar. The scroll consists of seventeen pieces of sheepskin sewn together into a single scroll and shows signs of being well used before it was stored away. The scroll comprises fifty-four columns of text that vary in width and average about twenty-nine lines of text per column. Measuring almost 24 feet in length and about 10 inches in height, 1QIsa[a] is the longest of the Qumran biblical scrolls. Its paragraphing system and intratextual divisions are elaborate and unlike those of the Masoretic Text. Through paleographic analysis, scholars date the scroll to about 125 BC. 1QIsa[a] represents a significant find because it includes all sixty-six chapters of Isaiah, except for minor lacunae, enabling scholars to conduct a complete study of this text. In contrast, the other Isaiah texts from Qumran, as fragmented and incomplete manuscripts,

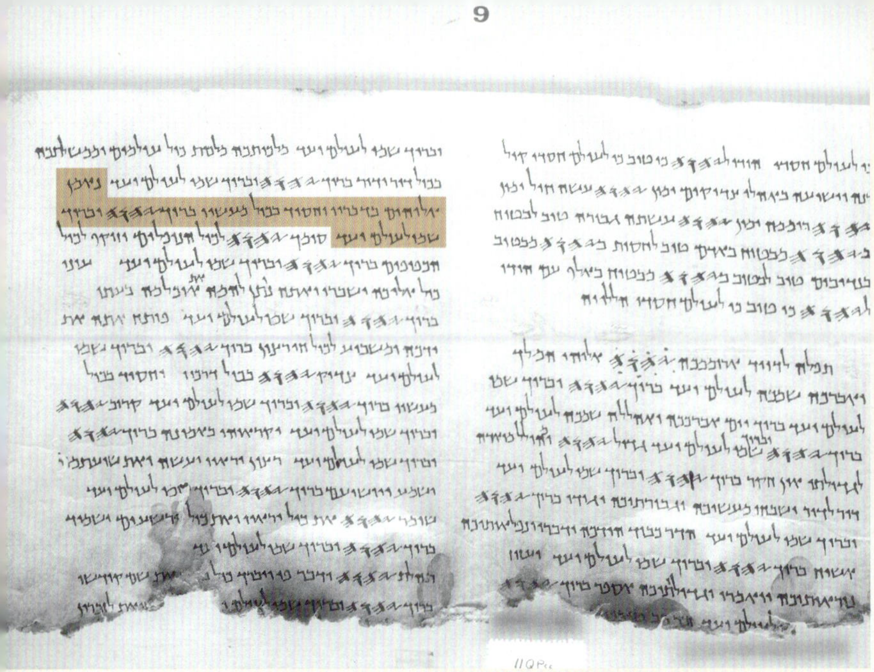

Psalm 145 begins after the line break on the right-hand column of the photo. The missing verse is highlighted in the left-hand column.

may slightly distort our understanding of Isaiah's textual history.

The Great Isaiah Scroll displays a number of scribal interventions in which the copyist or a subsequent scribe corrected readings or entered notations between the lines and in the margins. In addition, a comparison of 1QIsa[a] to the Masoretic Text reveals 1,400 variant readings, most of them minor. Most variants deal with orthography, or spelling (for example, color/colour, grey/gray), and taken as a whole, 1QIsa[a] displays a fuller orthography than the MT, meaning the scroll has more consonants in certain words. Some of the scroll's textual variants result from accidental errors that occurred during the transmission of the text by one or more generations of copyists. These include haplography, dittography, graphic similarity, misdivision of words, interchange of letters, and transposition of texts.

The Great Isaiah Scroll reflects the appearance of a biblical scroll at the time of Jesus and his apostles. It may have been similar in appearance to the Isaiah scroll that Jesus read from in the synagogue of Nazareth (see Luke 4:16–20).

This scroll is extremely important to the study of the Bible since it is approximately 1,000 years older than any other extant Hebrew copies of Isaiah. Although most of the readings of the scroll are the same as those of the traditional Hebrew Bible (the Masoretic Text), a number of important variant readings have been included in modern translations of Isaiah. For example, the King James translation of Isaiah 33:8 reads: "The highways lie waste, the wayfaring man ceaseth: he hath broken the covenant, he hath despised the cities, he regardeth no man." The Great Isaiah Scroll reads *witnesses* rather than *cities*: "The highways lie waste, the wayfaring man ceaseth: he hath broken the covenant, he hath despised the witnesses, he regardeth no man." Many scholars conclude that this presents a more accurate reading.

Discovery of a Missing Verse of Scripture

A verse of scripture missing from the Bible for about 2,000 years was rediscovered in the Psalms Scroll. This verse, from Psalm 145, reads as follows:

> God is faithful in all of his words,
> and pious in all of his deeds;
> blessed is the Lord
> and blessed is his name,
> forever,
> and ever.

Psalm 145 is an acrostic, or an ABC poem (written in the Hebrew language), meaning verse one begins with the first letter of the Hebrew alphabet, the second verse with the second letter of the alphabet, the third verse with the third letter, and so on through the entire alphabet. The missing verse, which begins with the Hebrew letter *nun* (roughly analogous to our English letter *n*), would have belonged between verses 13 and 14. There are twenty-two letters of the alphabet in Hebrew; therefore, the original Psalm 145 probably had twenty-two verses. However, Psalm 145 in the Old Testament contains only twenty-one verses. Cave 11 yielded the scroll that disclosed this verse.

Loving or Fearing God? A Controversial Word in Deuteronomy 8:6

A single word in Deuteronomy 8:6 profoundly changes the meaning of the verse. The traditional reading, based on medieval Hebrew manuscripts, is "And you shall keep the commandments of the LORD your God, by walking in his ways and by fearing him" (Deuteronomy 8:6 KJV). According to this passage, God's children were to keep his commandments by "walking in his ways" and "fearing him"; in other words, fear of God is a guiding principle. A copy of Deuteronomy from Qumran Cave 4, however, presents an important variant reading, for it states that God's children keep his commandments by "loving" him: "And you shall keep the commandments of the LORD your God, by walking in his ways and by loving him" (4QDeut[a] 8:6). *Love* and *fear* are two very different emotions and represent two distinct motivations for keeping God's commandments. The correct reading remains a controversial point.

Twenty-One Isaiah Scrolls

The discovery of twenty-one copies of Isaiah from the Judaean desert represents a singularly significant archaeological find. These Isaiah texts, discovered between the years 1947 and 1952, are written in ancient Hebrew and date between the years 175 BC and AD 70. Altogether, the Isaiah scrolls represent about 10 percent of all biblical scrolls discovered at Qumran. This statistic alone indicates that Isaiah held a prominent place in the Qumran

More than 500 different texts were found in Qumran Cave 4, including approximately 130 biblical texts.

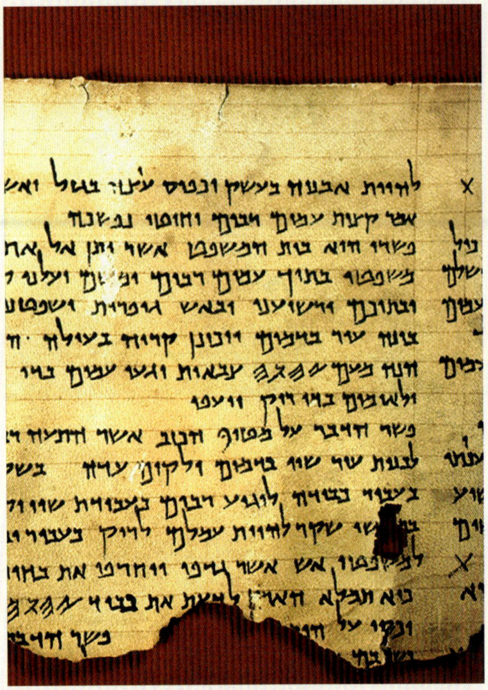

The Commentary of Habakkuk, column 10, reveals both horizontal and vertical rulings. Note how the scribe hung the Hebrew characters from the lines; in English, we align the bottom of the letters to the line below. Note also the Divine Name Jehovah in paleo-Hebrew script (see lines 7 and 14).

community, but other clues also reveal Isaiah's significance. Isaiah's book is treated as an authoritative work by the Qumran covenanters; in their sectarian writings, they cite, paraphrase, and allude to Isaiah more than to any other prophet. These Isaiah quotations and allusions are located in legal, eschatological, and poetic contexts of the sectarian writings and reveal ideological and theological positions of the Qumran community. In addition to the twenty-one Isaiah scrolls themselves and the sectarian writings that include quotations from and allusions to Isaiah, the Qumran discoveries included six Isaiah *pesharim* (commentaries).

While most of the Isaiah scrolls are damaged and fragmented because of long-term exposure to the elements, they influence our understanding of the textual history of the Bible in significant ways.

An ancient Bible

The Isaiah scrolls present a view of what biblical manuscripts looked like during the two centuries that preceded the Christian era.

One thousand years older

The Isaiah scrolls are consequential finds because they predate the medieval copies of the Hebrew Bible by approximately 1,000 years.

No chapters and verses

Unlike the medieval Hebrew Bible, with its consonantal and vocalization framework and system of notes, accents, chapters, and versification, the Isaiah scrolls feature handwritten manuscripts without chapters, versification, vowels, and accents.

Resources for Bible translation committees

The Isaiah scrolls provide new readings that apparently have been unknown to the world for approximately two millennia. Bible translation committees have incorporated a number of these new readings into modern translations.

Scribal conventions

The scribes' stylistic methods and conventions—including paragraphing and text divisions, marginal corrections and interlinear notations, and paleographic features—reveal the textual character of the Isaiah scrolls. Taken as a whole, these conventions disclose the nature of the scribal school that produced them. The Great Isaiah Scroll in particular presents a singular example of an ancient scroll that contains manifold scribal interventions.

Expanded understandings

The Isaiah scrolls are important texts for both academic and popular audiences because they expand understandings of the textual history of the Bible, especially for the book of Isaiah.

Orthography
The scrolls' assortment of orthographic features reveal much about spelling practices at the turn of the era, especially regarding the use of certain Hebrew consonants (in particular *waw, yod,* and *he*).

Producing New Copies of the Scriptures—Scribal Professionalism

The scrolls disclose much regarding the techniques, stylistic methods, and conventions of the ancient scribes as they prepared and copied the scrolls. Their careful and meticulous work indicates a high level of professionalism and competence as they copied and transmitted sacred texts from one generation to the next. As a matter of fact, those of us in the twenty-first century who love and appreciate the holy scriptures owe a great debt of gratitude to these scribes for their careful work. Scribal conventions include varying topics.

Horizontal and vertical rulings
The topic of rulings was discussed above in the section "What Did the Bible Look Like at the Time of Jesus Christ?"

Scrolls' overall lengths
The lengths of the scrolls vary according to their content. For example, the Temple Scroll consists of nineteen sheets of leather and is approximately 28 feet long; the Great Isaiah Scroll has seventeen sheets of leather and measures slightly longer than 23 feet. Leather sheet lengths vary from about 8 inches to 35 inches. Scholars have reconstructed the lengths of other scrolls.

Anciently, someone repaired a ripped segment of the Great Isaiah Scroll by (1) sewing it with linen thread (middle) and by (2) gluing a strip of leather to the back of the scroll. The glued leather (center bottom) is darker than the scroll.

Sense units
Scribal writing practices in the scrolls indicate a fully developed understanding of sense units, or small literary segments (we would call these sense units *sentences, paragraphs, chapters,* and the like). Although these early texts lacked both verse and chapter numbering arrangements (a much later development), the scribes set forth methods of identifying small and large sense units, poetical units, and entire books of scripture. To identify these units, scribes utilized special spacing techniques, including paragraphing and text divisions as well as marginal and interlinear notations.

Opisthographs and palimpsests
Most scrolls were written on one side of the leather or papyrus, but a few scrolls are opisthographs (written on both sides). A few palimpsests were also discovered

in the Qumran caves. (A palimpsest is a document that has been erased to make space for a new writing, but traces of the original writing remain.)

Handwriting styles
Handwriting styles differ among the scribes of various manuscripts; variations appear in letter and word dimensions as well as in scripts, which include square (Jewish) scripts, paleo-Hebrew scripts, and cryptic scripts.

Writing materials
The Qumran caves disclose details regarding writing materials (leather, papyrus, copper, and potsherds), ink (black, which is standard, and red, which is rare), inkwells, and styluses and other writing implements.

Various dimensions
The scrolls provide significant information regarding various dimensions: the sizes of columns and margins (top, bottom, and intercolumnar); the number of columns of written text on each leather sheet; the average number of lines per column (twenty lines of text); and the size of handle sheets (blank portions of leather at the beginning and ending of the scroll used for handling).

Miscellaneous items
The scrolls also provide other diverse bits of information: the production of scrolls; the manufacture of papyrus and leather; original composition titles; evidence of repairs, patching, and stitching of worn-out scrolls; correction and erasure procedures when the copyists made errors while copying the text; and the linen thread that tied the parchment sheets together.

A modern-day Jewish man writes on a papyrus scroll.

Jesus Christ, John the Baptist, and the New Testament

Since the discovery of the Dead Sea Scrolls in the late 1940s, many individuals have asked whether the scrolls contain references to Jesus Christ or John the Baptist; others have wondered if books or passages of the New Testament were discovered in the Qumran caves.

Jesus Christ

Most of the Qumran writings were written from the third to the first century BC, considerably before the advent of Christianity; they thus contain no historical references to Jesus Christ, to any of his apostles or disciples, or to Christianity. Before a great deal of information was known about the content of the scrolls, a few scholars suggested that Jesus Christ studied with the people of Qumran, but this suggestion is sensationalistic and without basis. Nor was he the Teacher of Righteousness, as some have claimed. Jesus Christ is not identified, explicitly or implicitly, in the nonbiblical scrolls. Nevertheless, the scrolls do provide much information about Judaism and the religious milieu of the period from which Christianity arose.

John the Baptist

No references to John the Baptist exist in the scrolls. Some scholars,[7] however, assert that John was affiliated with Qumran as he preached near the Jordan River, but sufficient evidence to prove this is lacking. Also, a few scholars have compared John's baptisms "in the wilderness" to the immersion rites of those at Qumran. However, John's baptisms were for "the remission of sins" (Mark 1:4), while the ritual of those at Qumran was for other purposes, as set forth in the Rule of the Community: "They shall not enter the water to partake of the pure Meal of the men of holiness, for they shall not be cleansed unless they turn from their wickedness."[8]

The New Testament

Not a single copy of a New Testament book was found among the Dead Sea Scrolls. The reason for this is twofold: first, the group who inhabited Qumran was *not* Christian; and second, most of the texts belonging to the corpus of the Dead Sea Scrolls were created and copied before the rise of Christianity in the first century AD.

Notwithstanding the complete lack of references to Jesus Christ or his followers, the Dead Sea Scrolls provide significant, illuminating material regarding the rise of Christianity for New Testament scholars.

Textual Variants: The Dead Sea Scrolls Bible versus the Masoretic Text

The readings of the Dead Sea Scrolls biblical texts usually accord with the Masoretic Text (MT) of the Hebrew Bible, but variant readings do appear. Most variant readings are minor and include plural versus singular forms; the use of conjunctions, prepositions, and definite articles; different morphological or lexical forms; and alternative verbal forms (aspects, tenses, active or passive voices, etc.). Far fewer in number are variant readings that pertain to content words, or those that change the text's meaning to a lesser or greater extent. Although such variants do exist among various manuscripts, they are not prominent enough to cause a loss of faith over a conflict of doctrine. To state it differently, variant readings that change the meaning of the text, either historically or theologically, are relatively infrequent.

In view of the ancient methods of transmitting texts by hand, sometimes in primitive conditions, and considering that the scribes lacked photocopy machines, computers, printing presses, and similar modern inventions, the Bible went through a remarkable process to make it into this century. In my opinion, the Dead Sea Scrolls Bible stands as a witness that the Old Testament has been passed down through the centuries with a respectable degree of accuracy. For this, we must be grateful to prophets, scribes, copyists, and everyone who was responsible for the Bible's transmission from generation to generation.

Despite the fact that the Dead Sea Scrolls biblical texts bring us 1,000 years closer to the original words of the prophets, we still do not have the so-called autograph texts—those that were penned by the prophets (or the scribes of the prophets) themselves. We possess apograph texts, which are copies (or copies of copies of copies) of the autograph texts. The apograph texts were created several hundred years after the autograph texts. Throughout the history of the texts of both the Old and the New Testaments, various errors (though mostly minor) have crept in—a fact that scholars have been aware of for centuries.

The forty-volume series *Discoveries in the Judaean Desert* from Oxford University Press sets forth both minor and major variants for each biblical text discovered in the Qumran caves. In this series, well-known and respectable biblical scholars have

The *Discoveries in the Judaean Desert* series (forty volumes) sets forth scholarly analyses on the Dead Sea Scrolls.

identified variant readings in the Hebrew witnesses of the Old Testament (that is, the Dead Sea Scrolls Bible, the Samaritan Pentateuch, and the Masoretic Text) or in the early translations (that is, the Greek Septuagint, the Latin Vulgate, or the Syriac Peshitta). Laypersons may consider consulting *The Dead Sea Scrolls Bible* translated by Abegg et al., which systematically sets forth variant readings, book by book; this work is an excellent resource, although it does not claim to be comprehensive. The best handbook that deals with biblical textual variants is Emanuel Tov's *Textual Criticism of the Hebrew Bible.*[9]

Scholars have identified various categories of errors. For example, "errors of the ear" are common in the text and may arise when the text is dictated to a scribe, or when the text is heard and not seen. An English example of such an error is the expression "you can see four miles," which may be heard as "you can see for miles." A common Hebrew error that falls in this category is the confusion of the word *lo* and the particle *lo'*, homophones that are translated respectively as "to him" or "no, not."

"Errors of the eye" may be the result of a scribe attempting to read the handwriting of an earlier scribe, whose book hand is sometimes illegible or who used an archaic script. Such errors include the confusion of similar-looking letters. In English, letters whose appearance is similar include *m* and *n*, *b* and *d*, *o* and *c*, *u* and *v*, *v* and *w*, or *v* and *y*. Likewise, some letters in the Hebrew alphabet appear similar. Another scribal error results from the incorrect dividing of letters and words. An English example illustrates this concept: the letters *Godisnowhere,* designed to be read "God is now here," may be misread as "God is nowhere."

Below are illustrative examples of textual variants from 1 Samuel 1. The first two examples are considered minor variants; the last three are more significant.

1 Samuel 1:11
"no razor will go up on his head" (MT)

"no razor will pass over his head" (Dead Sea Scrolls)

1 Samuel 1:13
"And Hannah, she spoke" (MT)

"And she spoke" (Dead Sea Scrolls)

1 Samuel 1:22
Not in MT

"I will offer him as a nazarite all the days of his life" (Dead Sea Scrolls)

1 Samuel 1:23
Elkanah tells Hannah: "Do what seems best to you, wait until you have weaned him, only, may the Lord establish his word." (MT)

Elkanah tells Hannah: "Do what seems best to you, wait until you have weaned him, only, may the Lord establish that which goes out of your mouth." (Dead Sea Scrolls)

1 Samuel 1:24
"When she had weaned him, she took him up with her, along with three bulls" (MT)

"When she had weaned him, she took him up with her, along with a three year old bull" (Dead Sea Scrolls)

Scholars employ scientific methods in their quest to determine which of the textual variants are original and which are secondary, although at times it is difficult to draw a firm conclusion.

A scribe corrects a scroll

"The scribe of [the Great Isaiah Scroll] was not one of the best. He made many mistakes, most of which, though, he himself discovered and corrected. . . However, several passages that were omitted by this scribe were later inserted by another, as is indicated by the different handwriting."

Yigael Yadin, *The Message of the Scrolls* (New York Crossroad, 1992) 85.

Even after the invention of the printing press, errors are known to exist in different printings of the Bible. The first edition of the King James Version (KJV), printed in 1611, contained a number of errors, some of which were corrected in the 1612 edition, followed by additional corrections and changes in the 1613 edition. For instance, the 1611 edition read "then cometh Judas" instead of "then cometh Jesus" (Matthew 26:36); "strain out a gnat" rather than the correct "strain at a gnat" (Matthew 23:24); and "approved to death" in place of "appointed to death" (1 Corinthians 4:9).

Other editions have been named after major errors that have crept into the text. The so-called Wicked Bible was named because the term *not* was omitted in the seventh of the Ten Commandments, thus reading "Thou shalt commit adultery"; the Unrighteous Bible received its title because it stated that the *unrighteous* would inherit the kingdom of God; and the Vinegar Bible sets forth the parable of the vinegar rather than the parable of the vineyard. Fortunately, most printing press changes are fairly insignificant and deal with spelling changes or minor variant readings; only a few relate to historical or theological issues.

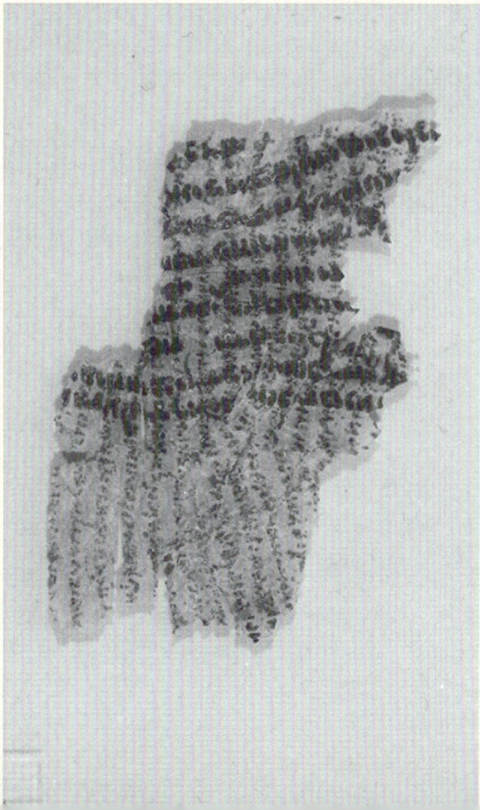

A fragment of a phylactery from Cave 4. A scribe wrote words on both sides of the document; note the bleed of ink from the opposite side of the papyrus.

Ancient Phylacteries and Mezuzot—Symbols of the Jewish Faith

The Dead Sea Scrolls include very early examples of phylacteries and *mezuzot*, important symbols of the Jews. Phylacteries (see Matthew 23:5), or *tefillin* (singular, *tefillah*), are small, leather boxes attached to cords that are bound to the head and left arm. Within the boxes are very small parchments containing verses from Exodus and Deuteronomy (usually including Exodus 13:1–16; and Deuteronomy 6:4–9; 11:13–21), although some of the *tefillin* of Qumran also included the Ten Commandments. The idea of *tefillin* originates from Deuteronomy 6:8, which reads, "bind them for a sign upon thine hand, and they shall be as frontlets between thine eyes." Approximately thirty *tefillin* have been found in the various caves of the Judaean Desert.

Mezuzot (singular, *mezuzah*) are small boxes or containers attached to the right side of the doorpost of a house. Each box contains a parchment with passages from Deuteronomy (usually 6:4–9 and 11:13–21), although the Qumran collection sometimes contained the Ten Commandments.

The tradition of *mezuzot* originated from a command of Deuteronomy 6:9: "Thou shalt write them upon the posts of thy house, and on thy gates." Several *mezuzot* texts have been found among the scrolls.

A religious Jew wears phylacteries on his forehead and arm during prayer.

Bible-like (Parabiblical) Texts Otherwise Unknown

New Writings about Ancient Prophets and Other Characters

The Qumran caves yielded several compositions that are generally affiliated with well-known Old Testament characters such as Daniel, Enoch, Ezekiel, Jacob, Joseph, Joshua, Judah, Levi, Moses, Naphtali, Noah, Rachel, and Samuel. Many of these writings were unknown to the modern world prior to their discovery. Modern scholars have provided names for these texts, which include the following: Book of Noah, Daniel Apocryphon, Discourse on the Exodus/Conquest Tradition, Elisha Apocryphon, Enoch, Genesis Apocryphon, Jeremiah Apocryphon, Joshua Apocryphon, Jubilees, Moses Apocryphon, Naphtali, Prayer of Enosh, Pseudo-Daniel, Pseudo-Ezekiel, Reworked Pentateuch, Temple Scroll, Testament of Jacob, Testament of Joseph, Testament of Judah, Testament of Qohath, Testament of Levi, Text concerning Rachel and Joseph, Text Mentioning the Flood, Visions of Amram, Visions of Samuel, and Words of Michael.

Scholars refer to these compositions as parabiblical, pseudepigraphic, or apocryphal texts. Most of these texts constitute a retelling of biblical narratives and passages, although some of them have interpretative or periphrastic elements. Many of these texts introduce new biblical themes and subject matter. For example,

Rolled-up Genesis Apocryphon scroll with end views and fragments.

Book of Enoch fragment from Cave 4. Biblical texts reveal very little about Enoch, but Enoch is a prominent character in the Dead Sea Scrolls.

Words of Moses fragments from Cave 1. Moses admonishes ancient Israel to keep God's commandments.

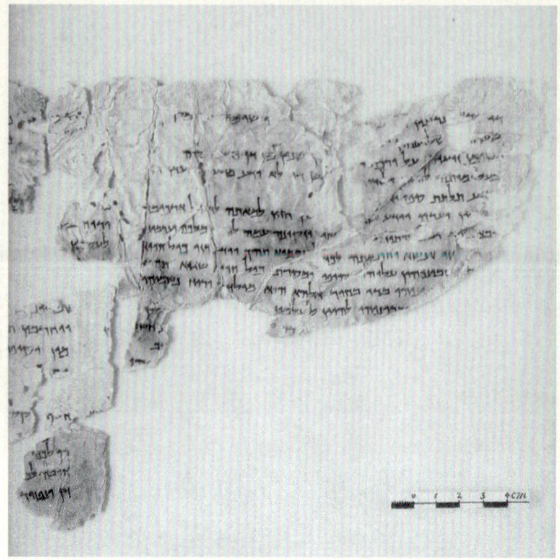

Birth of Noah fragment. Several texts from Qumran are associated with the prophet Noah; some scholars claim that these texts were part of a book of Noah that existed in antiquity.

the Genesis Apocryphon retells and amplifies many of the events recorded in Genesis, including the following three examples:

1. *Sarai's extraordinary beauty*. Regarding Sarai's personal appearance, the book of Genesis simply states: "when Abram was come into Egypt, the Egyptians beheld the woman [Sarai] that she was very fair" (Genesis 12:14). The Genesis Apocryphon, however, adds numerous details regarding Sarai's extraordinary beauty. "[How] beautiful is her face! How . . . fine are the hairs of her head! How lovely are her eyes! How desirable her nose and all the radiance of her countenance . . . how beautiful all her whiteness! How pleasing are her arms and how perfect her hands, and how [desirable] all the appearance of her hands! How fair are her palms and how long and slender are her fingers! How comely are her feet, how perfect her thighs! No virgin or bride led into the marriage chamber is more beautiful than she; she is fairer than all other women. Truly, her beauty is greater than theirs. Yet together with all this grace she possesses abundant wisdom, so that whatever she does is perfect."[1]

2. *The laying on of hands*. According to the Genesis Apocryphon, God scourged Pharaoh and his household because Pharaoh had taken Sarai, Abraham's wife, for evil purposes: "The Most High God sent a spirit to scourge [Pharaoh] . . . it scourged him and all his household. And he was unable to approach [Sarai], and although he was with her for two years, he knew her not." After two years, the scourge not only continued, but it intensified. Pharaoh sought help from his advisors, healers, and wizards, but they were unsuccessful. Finally, Abraham approached Pharaoh. Abraham recalls, "So I prayed [for him] . . . and I laid my hands on his [head]; and the scourge departed from him and the

evil [spirit] was expelled [from him], and he lived."[2]

3. *The magnitude of the promised land.* The Genesis Apocryphon provides many details beyond those in the biblical book of Genesis regarding the boundaries and size of the land promised to Abraham and his descendants.[3]

Unfortunately, we lack knowledge of how the people of Qumran themselves classified these Bible-like texts. Were they inspired commentaries? Were they texts written by a community leader or prominent teacher? Did these texts possess religious authority equal to the canonical works of the Bible? Regardless of how these texts were viewed by their owners, they offer scholars a treasure chest of information into the religious world of the Jews who owned them.

The Enigmatic Temple Scroll

Many of the compositions found among the Dead Sea Scrolls were unknown to the modern reader prior to their discovery in the caves; such texts included a number of parabiblical texts, or texts that are Bible-like in character. The Temple Scroll, discovered in Cave 11 in 1956, is one such text. In fact, the scroll's passages often parallel those from Exodus, Leviticus, and Deuteronomy. About 28 feet in length, the Temple Scroll is the longest of the scrolls. Its paleography dates it to between 150 BC to AD 1, although it may have been originally composed at a much earlier date.

This scroll is highly significant because it claims to reveal the temple that will be built in Jerusalem in the last days, or the eschatological period. The scroll examines various aspects of the temple complex, construction, and functions; it describes and provides the measurements of the sanctuary and its holy of holies, chambers and colonnades, mercy seat, cherubim, veil, table, golden lamp, altar, and courtyards.

The architecture and structure of this temple is very different from Solomon's temple and the temple described in Ezekiel 40–46, for the Temple Scroll describes three concentric courts—an inner, middle, and outer court. These three courts delineate three levels of holiness for temple officiators, workers, and worshippers. The innermost court of the temple was the most holy, and as one moved outward the courts (and the respective ordinances or rituals performed therein) decreased in holiness. This approach to hierarchical sanctity follows the model of the Mosaic tabernacle and Solomon's temple, which also followed the pattern of concentric spheres of holiness.

The Temple Scroll goes beyond the physical features of the temple to describe the ideal temple society and its covenant with God. The scroll characterizes sacrifices, regulations of purity, and officers affiliated with the temple. It outlines laws relating to idolatry and apostasy; vows and oaths; priests, Levites, and priestly dues; witnesses; sacrificial animals; conduct during war; the rebellious son; and crimes punishable by hanging. Many of the laws in this text pertain to the ritual purity of the temple worshippers.

The temple was to serve as a reminder of the awesome presence of God and the purity necessary to approach him. This temple of the last days, as set forth in the scroll, was to preserve a stricter ritual purity among the people. The laws governing the sanctity of the edifice were more restrictive than those pertaining to

The Temple Scroll, the longest of the scrolls (approximately 28 feet in length), has many Bible-like qualities, which makes it somewhat mysterious to modern readers.

other Israelite temples, thereby lifting the entire level of the community to a higher state of purity.

The scroll does not simply repeat the laws on social conduct and temple worship as they appear in the books of Exodus, Leviticus, Numbers, and Deuteronomy: it blends them into a new, harmonious whole, sometimes adding new materials such as festivals of new oil and wine that are not mentioned in the law of Moses. The Lord says of his covenant people and this temple, "I shall accept them and they shall be my people and I shall be for them for ever. I will dwell with them for ever and ever and will sanctify my [sa]nctuary by my glory. I will cause my glory to rest on it until the day of creation on which I shall create my sanctuary, establishing it for myself for all time according to the covenant which I have made with Jacob in Bethel."[4]

An important question regarding this scroll is, how much religious authority did the Jews who possessed the Temple Scroll assign to it? Yigael Yadin, who wrote a three-volume work on the Temple Scroll, has attributed significant religious authority to the scroll; he wrote that the scroll is "a veritable Torah of the Lord."[5]

The Seductress

A composition that scholars have named The Seductress pertains to a woman who uses her wiles to seduce others into participating in sexual sin (some scholars call this text Wiles of a Wicked Woman). The poem belongs to a genre called Wisdom literature, a literary genre that is also found in the biblical books of Psalms, Proverbs, and Ecclesiastes.

Using poetic language, this composition refers to several of the seductress's body parts, including her lips, heart, kidneys, eyes, hands, and legs. For example, "Her *heart* is set up as a snare, and her *kidneys* (affections) as a fowler's nets. Her *eyes* are defiled with iniquity, her *hands* have seized hold of the Pit. Her *legs* go down to work wickedness."[6] The composition also refers to her skirts, clothes, veils, ornaments (that is, jewelry), and beds.

Similar to harlots of old, the seductress positions herself in places where she can tempt those who pass by: "In the city's squares she veils herself, and she stands at the gates of towns."[7] As a seductress, she employs sweet talk to those who will listen: "She is ever prompt to oil her words, and she flatters with irony."[8] A portion of The Seductress appears here:

> She is the beginning of all the
>   ways of iniquity.
> Woe [and] disaster to all who
>   possess her!
> And desolation to all who hold her!
> For her ways are ways of death,
> and her paths are roads of sin,
> and her tracks are pathways to
>   iniquity,
> and her by-ways are rebellious
>   wrong-doings.
> Her gates are gates of death,
> and from the entrance of the
>   house
> she sets out towards the under-
>   world.
> None of those who enter there will
>   ever return,
> and all who possess her will de-
>   scend to the Pit.
> She lies in wait in secret places.[9]

The cited portion of the poem reveals that disaster will come upon those who are enticed into sexual sin. The poem features a series of parallelisms that recall similar structures in various biblical psalms and hymns. In the first parallelism shown above (lines two and three), *disaster* corresponds with *desolation*, and *all who possess her* parallels *all who hold her*. In the second parallelism (lines four and five), *her ways* is analogous to *her paths*, and *ways of death* parallels *roads of sin*. In the third parallelism (lines six and seven), *her tracks* and *her by-ways* are comparable, and *iniquity* and *wrong-doings* are corresponding elements. In yet another parallelism (lines eight and nine), *gates* corresponds with *entrance*, and *death* is parallel to *underworld*.

This poem has multiple layers to it. Not only does it set forth a sexual temptress, but the seductress also serves as a metaphor of a person or a group who seeks to draw others away from the truth. As one scholar explained, this text "represents the female figure as much more than a temptation to lead a life contrary to the tenets of wisdom; she has become, rather, the personification of an antagonistic group, and the central controversy has evolved into the author's concern for the correct fulfillment of the entire Torah."[10]

Beatitudes—A Fascinating and Previously Unknown Text

Qumran Cave 4 yielded a fascinating if not perplexing text called Beatitudes (4Q525). In Beatitudes, wisdom is personified as a woman, and those who hold fast to her are blessed. The last two lines provide a summary of how a person actually attains the lady called Wisdom; he/she does so by "walk[ing] in the Law of the Most High." A portion of Beatitudes reads:

Blessed are those who hold to her
(Wisdom's) precepts
and do not hold to the ways of
iniquity.
Blessed are those who rejoice in
her,
and do not burst forth in ways of
folly.
Blessed are those who seek her
with pure hands,
and do not pursue her with a
treacherous heart.
Blessed is the man who has
attained Wisdom,
and walks in the Law of the Most
High.
He directs his heart towards her
ways,
and restrains himself by her
corrections,
and always takes delight in her
chastisements.[11]

This composition recalls three literary types that belong to the ancient world:

1. Beatitudes begins several clauses with the formula *Blessed*, a structure similar to Jesus's Beatitudes that were delivered on the Sermon on the Mount (Matthew 5:3–11; see also Psalm 1:1).

2. In Beatitudes, wisdom is personified as a woman (the word *wisdom* in Hebrew, *hokmah*, is a feminine noun), and those who hold her, seek her with pure hands, and attain her are those who walk in God's law. Personifying wisdom in Beatitudes recalls Proverbs 8, where wisdom is also set forth as a woman: "Doth not wisdom cry? and understanding put forth her voice? She standeth in the top of high places, by the way in the places of the paths. She crieth at the gates, at the entry of the city," and so on (Proverbs 8:1–3 KJV).

3. Beatitudes was written in a beautiful form of biblical poetry called parallelism, where each set of two lines parallels or corresponds with each other. Similar parallelistic structures are located in the books of Psalms, Proverbs, Isaiah, and elsewhere. In Beatitudes, the parallelisms sometimes have antithetical features, or contrasting thoughts, such as (*Wisdom*'s) precepts versus *iniquity*, or *pure hands* and *treacherous heart*. The parallelisms also feature synonymous elements; *Wisdom* corresponds with the *Law of the Most High*, and *her corrections* corresponds with *her chastisements*.

These beautiful and inspired Beatitudes remain a puzzle. Were they once part of an ancient bible together with Psalms, Proverbs, Ecclesiastes and other books belonging to the Wisdom literature genre? Did the ancient Israelites or Jews consider them to be canonical and to have religious authority?

Messianic Apocalypse

Scholars have named a composition from Cave 4 the Messianic Apocalypse because it mentions a Messiah; they also call it a resurrection fragment because line 12 refers to the resurrection—"For He will heal the wounded, and revive the dead." The composition has particular import because it may shed further light on how the Qumran community viewed the Messiah. Dated to the first century BC, the text is very fragmented (11 or more fragments), which means that our understanding of its content remains incomplete. Fragment 2, the largest of the fragments, reads:

. . . [the heav]ens and earth will listen to His Messiah and none therein will stray from the commandments of the holy ones.
Seekers of the Lord, strengthen yourselves in His service!
All you hopeful in (your) heart, will you not find the Lord in this?
For the Lord will consider the pious (*hasidim*) and call the righteous by name.
Over the poor His spirit will hover and will renew the faithful with His power.
And He will glorify the pious on the throne of the eternal Kingdom.
He who liberates the captives, restores sight to the blind, straightens the b[ent] (Ps. cxlvi, 7–8).
And f[or] ever I will clea[ve to the h]opeful and in His mercy . . .
And the fr[uit . . .] will not be delayed for anyone
And the Lord will accomplish glorious things which have never been as [He . . .]
For He will heal the wounded, and revive the dead and bring good news to the poor (Isa. lxi, 1).
. . . He will lead the uprooted and knowledge . . . and smoke (?).[12]

This text reveals the following four noteworthy themes:

1. The word *Messiah* is located in the first line; *Messiah* is preceded with the personal possessive pronoun *his* ("his Messiah"), although we lack the antecedent of *his*. The Messiah is not identified.

2. The word Lord (*Adonai*), used four times, is a significant content word. The four attestations are: "Seekers of the Lord"; "All you hopeful in (your) heart, will you not find the Lord in this?"; "For the Lord will consider the pious (*hasidim*) and call the righteous by name"; "the Lord will accomplish glorious things which have never been."

3. Either citing or paraphrasing a portion of Psalm 146:6–7, the Messianic Apocalypse reads: "He who liberates the captives, restores sight to the blind, straightens the b[ent]." These words recall Psalm 146:7–8: "The LORD looseth the prisoners: The LORD openeth the eyes of the blind: the LORD raiseth them that are bowed down" (KJV).

4. Similarly, Messianic Apocalypse either cites or paraphrases a portion of Isaiah 66:1. The scroll reads: "For He will heal the wounded, and revive the dead and bring good news to the poor." These further words call to mind Isaiah 61:1: "The Spirit of the Lord God is upon me; because the LORD hath anointed me to preach good tidings unto the meek; he hath sent me to bind up the brokenhearted, to proclaim liberty to the captives, and the opening of the prison to them that are bound." We recall also that Jesus Christ cited this verse from Isaiah in the synagogue in Nazareth (see Luke 4:16–18).

Qumran scholar Émile Puech sums up the historical significance of the composition under discussion: "A few of the fragments of the Hebrew Messianic

Apocalypse (4Q521) manuscript have a great importance for the history of religions."[13]

Previously Unknown Psalms

The Psalms Scroll is a magnificent example of a manuscript that belonged to the world of antiquity. This famous scroll, discovered in Cave 11, contains many of the same psalms that are part of the book of Psalms in the Bible; of this scroll's forty-nine psalms, forty also appear in the Bible. However, the ordering of the psalms in the Psalms Scroll is somewhat different from that in the Bible.

Similar to the biblical book of Psalms, the Psalms Scroll contains a collection of hymns and songs that were expressed by one or more Jewish communities on occasions of worship, reflection, and devotion. Many of these psalms constitute praises about God and his majesty, omnipotence, love, and mercy. For this reason the Hebrew word for the book of Psalms is *Tehillim*, which means "[songs of] praises."

Although the biblical book of Psalms contains 150 psalms, the evidence of the Psalms Scroll indicates that anciently many more psalms were in existence. According to this scroll, King David composed a great number of psalms and songs:

> David son of Jesse . . . wrote 3,600 psalms and 364 songs to sing before the altar for the daily perpetual sacrifice, for all the days of the year; and 52 songs for the Sabbath offerings; and 30 songs for the New Moons, for Feast-days and for the Day of Atonement. In all, the songs which he uttered were 446, and 4 songs to make music on behalf of those stricken (by evil spirits). In all, they were 4,050.

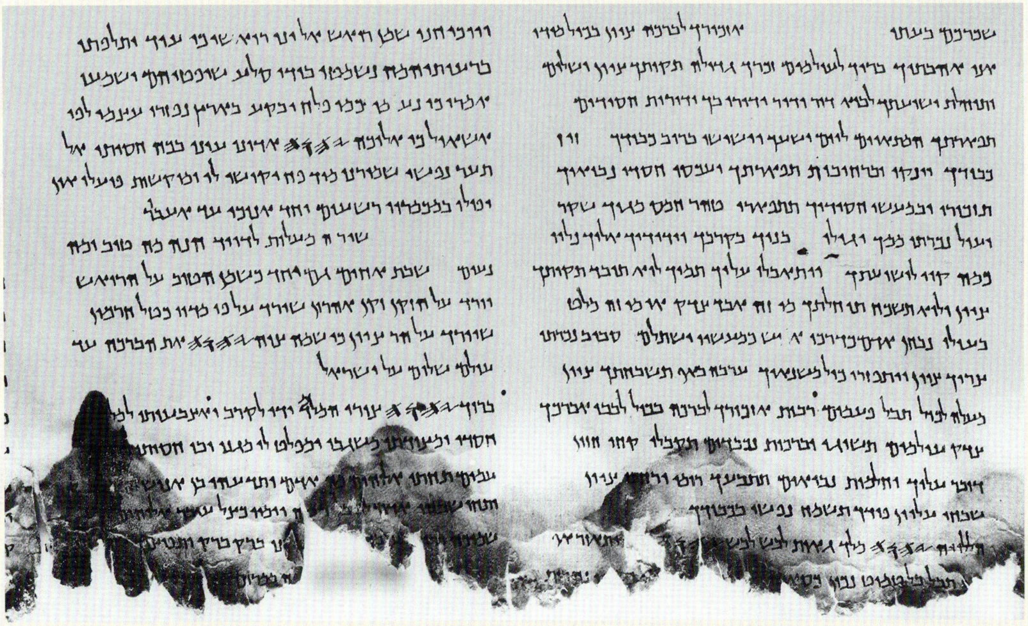

The Psalms Scroll contains several noncanonical psalms, including the Apostrophe to Zion, where Zion is addressed as if it were a woman.

All these he uttered through prophecy which was given him from before the Most High.[14]

In addition to the forty biblical psalms, the Psalms Scroll includes previously unknown compositions. Scholars have named these new compositions Plea for Deliverance, Apostrophe to Zion, Hymn to the Creator, David's Last Words, and David's Compositions. The Psalms Scroll also includes Psalm 151, which was already known to exist in the Septuagint (Greek translation of the Bible) but is lacking in the Hebrew Bible. This psalm pertains to David the shepherd, his musical talents, his call from the Lord, and his defeat of Goliath.

The fact that these previously unknown psalms appear on the leather scroll together with the canonical psalms (those psalms belonging to the Bible) has encouraged some scholars to speculate that these additional psalms held a degree of canonical or religious authority for those who owned the scroll. This, of course, remains a matter of speculation and controversy.

A portion of the noncanonical psalm Hymn to the Creator is presented here:

The Lord is great and holy,
the Most Holy for generation after
generation.
Majesty goes before him,
and after him abundance of many
waters.
Loving-kindness and truth are
about his face;
truth and judgement and righteousness are the pedestal of his
throne.
He divides light from obscurity;
he establishes the dawn by the
knowledge of his heart.
When all his angels saw it, they
sang,
for he showed them that which
they had not known.
He crowns the mountains with
fruit,
with good food for all the living.[15]

This psalm, similar to many of the canonical psalms of the Bible, features symbolic forms, figures of speech, and parallelisms. A portion of another noncanonical psalm, Apostrophe to Zion is also presented here:

I will remember you, O Zion, for a
blessing;
with all my might I love you;
your memory is to be blessed for
ever.
Your hope is great, O Zion;
Peace and your awaited salvation
will come.
Generation after generation shall
dwell in you,
and generations of the pious shall
be your ornament.
They who desire the day of your
salvation
shall rejoice in the greatness of
your glory.
They shall be suckled on the fullness of your glory,
and in your beautiful streets they
shall make tinkling sounds.
You shall remember the pious
deeds of your prophets,
and shall glorify yourselves in the
deeds of your pious ones.
Cleanse violence from your midst;
lying and iniquity, may they be cut
off from you.
Your sons shall rejoice within you,
and your cherished ones shall be
joined to you.

The Psalms Scroll

"The scroll is tanned animal skin, deep yellow to brown in hue, considerably darker than the infra-red photographs would indicate. It lacks little of being 1 mm. thick. It is exceptional in this regard, and P. W. Skehan has suggested it may be calf skin rather than the accustomed goat skin of Qumrân."

J. A. Sanders, "Introduction: A. Data, Contents, and Index," in DJD IV, 3.

How much they have hoped in
your salvation,
and how much your perfect ones
have mourned for you?
Your hope, O Zion, shall not
perish,
and your expectation will not be
forgotten.[16]

In this beautiful psalm, Zion is addressed as if she is a person: "I will remember you, O Zion . . . Your hope is great, O Zion." Note also the many wonders and glories associated with Zion: "the greatness of your glory"; "the fullness of your glory"; "your beautiful streets"; both "lying and iniquity" are cut off from Zion; and "Your hope, O Zion, shall not perish, and your expectation shall not be forgotten."

Do Any of the Parabiblical Texts Have Biblical Authority?

Most or all major Christian faiths maintain that the Hebrew protocanonical books (which include the books of Genesis, Exodus, Leviticus, Numbers, and so forth) have religious, canonical authority. However, various Christian faiths have different understandings regarding which apocryphal or deuterocanonical books belong to the Old Testament. For example, the Western tradition (e.g., Protestant and Roman Catholic), Eastern Orthodox tradition (e.g., Greek Orthodox, Slavonic Orthodox, and Georgian Orthodox), Oriental Orthodox tradition (e.g., Armenian Apostolic, Syriac Orthodox, and Coptic Orthodox), and Assyrian Eastern tradition (e.g., Assyrian Church of the East) make their own assessment of which additional books beyond the Hebrew protocanonical books belong to the Old Testament. These traditions may include in their respective Bibles one or more of the following writings: Tobit, Judith, 1–4 Maccabees, Book of Wisdom, Sirach, Psalm 151, Baruch, Prayer of Manasseh, and Letter of Jeremiah, as well as additions to Esther and Daniel.

With the coming forth of the various Dead Sea Scrolls parabiblical texts, scholars in recent decades have reassessed the meaning of the canon. They have questioned the scriptural authority of these and other texts that have certain Bible-like qualities, even though these texts do *not* exist in our version of the Holy Bible.[17] For example, Emanuel Tov, editor in chief of the International Team of Translators of the Dead Sea Scrolls, has written that "the definition of the scope of the biblical corpus is unclear. . . . The list is limited to the texts which subsequently came to be included in Hebrew Scripture, while the boundaries of that group in the last centuries (165) BCE and the first centuries CE remain open to debate. . . . The notion of what exactly constitutes a biblical scroll is not always clear."[18] One recent publication addresses the issue of canonicity head-on. In his article "Questions of Canon Viewed through the Dead Sea Scrolls," Qumran scholar James C. VanderKam begins with these words: "As nearly as we can tell, there was no canon of scripture in Second Temple Judaism. That is, before 70 C.E. no authoritative body of which we know drew up a list of books that alone were regarded as supremely authoritative, a list from which none could be subtracted and to which none could be added."[19]

After setting the background and context for his article, VanderKam presents the direction that he will take: "The thesis that I would like to defend regarding the second temple period is that while there were authoritative writings, and these were at times gathered into recognizable groupings (for example, Law, Prophets, Others), the category of revealed literature was not considered a closed and fixed one, at least not for the type of Judaism for which we now have the most evidence—the people of the Dead Sea Scrolls."[20] VanderKam then examines three individual compositions—Reworked Pentateuch, the Temple Scroll, and Jubilees—in light of the possibility that these three may have had scriptural status to the Jews who possessed them. All three of these compositions fit textual forms of scripture—they read more or less like scripture. The Temple Scroll, writes VanderKam, "reproduces pentateuchal material and generally has a known form of scriptural text,"[21] as do the other two compositions under discussion.

Scholars do not know which writings from Qumran were considered to be scripture or to hold canonical authority to the Jews who possessed them (the Essenes, according to most scholars). Because of this, several questions remain with regard to those who possessed these scrolls: What books constituted their bible or scriptural canon? Did they consider other books, beyond those in the Old Testament, to have canonical authority? Although it is quite probable that these Jews accepted all the books of the Old Testament as biblical and canonical, it is also possible that they accepted other books into their canon of scripture—books such as the Temple Scroll, 1 Enoch, Jubilees, some of the apocryphal psalms, the Beatitudes, and others.[22]

Three notable Qumran scholars of our present day—Martin Abegg, Peter Flint, and Eugene Ulrich—include five texts in *The Dead Sea Scrolls Bible* that have not traditionally belonged to the Old Testament. These five are Jubilees, 1 Enoch, Ben Sira (Sirach), Tobit, and the Epistle of Jeremiah. According to the introduction of *The Dead Sea Scrolls Bible*, "It is . . . most likely that the Qumran community viewed the books of 1 Enoch and Jubilees as Scripture."[23]

The Dead Sea Scrolls Bible, also called the Qumran Bible, consists of texts found among the Dead Sea Scrolls that appear in the modern Hebrew Bible or Christian Old Testament. Neither expression—Dead Sea Scrolls Bible or Qumran Bible—may adequately express the contents of the bible used by the Jews who owned this collection of religious texts. We simply do not know which texts they considered to have religious or canonical authority or which books they included among their sacred texts. Their bible may have had a greater or lesser number of texts than we have in the Holy Bible.

VanderKam provides an appropriate summary of how we should view the apocryphal and parabiblical books of Qumran: "In view of the evidence from Qumran, we should avoid using the words *Bible* and *biblical* for this period and this community. This is not to deny that group had authoritative writings; the difficulty is that we . . . cannot always be sure which of those writings were authoritative and which were not."[24]

Texts of the Jewish Sect

Who Wrote or Possessed the Dead Sea Scrolls?

No one today knows who wrote or possessed the Dead Sea Scrolls, although several hypotheses, based on both literary and archaeological evidences, exist.

Essene hypothesis
This is the majority view (see below).

Sadducean hypothesis
The Sadducean legal system and set of doctrines often parallel the positions set forth in the sectarian scrolls.

Jewish-Christian hypothesis
A few of the teachings of the sectarian scrolls are aligned, more or less, with those of Christians.

Jerusalem hypothesis
The Qumran settlement had nothing to do with a Jewish sect because Qumran may have been a military fortress. The scrolls stored in nearby caves may have been transported from a library in Jerusalem and hidden in the caves before the Romans conquered Jerusalem in AD 70.

After the scrolls were removed from the Qumran caves, they were initially housed in the Rockefeller Museum (*left*), East Jerusalem.

Josephus, a first-century-AD Jewish military leader and historian, describes a variety of Jewish groups active in the last centuries BC and the first centuries AD, including the Boethusians, Essenes, Pharisees, Sadducees, and Zealots. From contemporary and near-contemporary accounts of the beliefs and practices of these Jewish groups, scholars have noted similarities between the descriptions of these groups and the writings in the Dead Sea Scrolls. Two groups, in particular, have received attention as potential candidates for the inhabitants of Qumran: the Sadducees and the Essenes.

A number of scholars believe that the writers of the Dead Sea Scrolls were Sadducees or proto-Sadducees. This judgment is based on certain similarities between the teachings of the Sadducees and the writings of the sectarian texts of the Dead Sea Scrolls, especially in material found in the letter now known as MMT (Some Observances of the Law). Others, however, have noted that the points of comparison are not particularly strong.

Most scholars are of the opinion that the writers and owners of the scrolls were Essenes; they base their arguments on a comparison of the scrolls with the writings of the Jewish historian Josephus and other ancient sources, including Philo, Pliny, and Hippolytus. These sources, taken together with the archaeological data from Qumran, present a description of the Essenes and their belief system:

- avoidance of spitting
- belief in an afterlife
- belief in angels
- belief in healing the sick
- beliefs in prophets and prophecy
- celibacy (perhaps for some, although this subject is controversial)
- common meal
- communal practices
- geographical location
- reading books and learning
- rituals, including purificatory washings with water
- sharing of property
- strict rules regarding the admission to the community
- strict Sabbath observance
- study of the law
- submission to the community's leaders
- years that the Essene community existed at Qumran

Furthermore, Pliny the Elder, a Roman writer, made the following statement regarding the Essenes:

> To the west [of the Dead Sea] the Essenes have put the necessary distance between themselves and the insalubrious shore. They are a people unique of its kind and admirable beyond all others in the whole world without women and renouncing love entirely, without money, and having for company only the palm trees. Owing to the throng of newcomers, this people is daily reborn in equal number; indeed, those whom, wearied by the fluctuations of fortune, life leads to adopt their customs, stream in in great numbers. Thus, unbelievable though this may seem, for thousands of centuries a race has existed which is eternal yet into which no one is born: so fruit-

What happened to the Essenes?

"Whether the Essenes in whole or in part fled their settlement with the approach of the Romans, or were trapped in Qumrân and slaughtered, we cannot know with certainty. At all events the Essenes were prevented from carrying away their manuscripts, with the result that their library, abandoned in nearby caves, survived. Ironically, had the community survived, the manuscripts no doubt would have perished."

The strictness of the Essenes

"Josephus informs us that the Essenes observed the Sabbath so strictly that they prepared all food in advance and did not move any vessels: 'Moreover, they are stricter than any other of the Jews in resting from their labors on the seventh day; for they not only get their food ready the day before, that they may not be obligated to kindle a fire on that day, but they will not remove any vessel out of its place' (*War* 2.147; Whiston's translation)."

Jodi Magnes, *Stone and Dung, Oil and Spit: Jewish Daily Life in the Time of Jesus* (Grand Rapids, MI: Eerdmans, 2011), 85.

> ful for them is the repentance which others feel for their past lives! Below the Essenes was the town of Engada [Engedi], which yielded only to Jerusalem in fertility and palm-groves but is today become another ash-heap. From there, one comes to the fortress of Masada, situated on a rock, and itself near the Dead Sea (Lake of Asphalt).[1]

Although this brief passage by Pliny may contain factual or historical errors, its details about the Essenes parallel ideas found in the scrolls: renouncing money, experiencing an increase in converts to the sect, and the long existence of the group. Pliny's statement also places the Essene's geographical location at or near Qumran. His comments can, of course, still be interpreted in more than one way, making positive identification of the inhabitants of Qumran nearly impossible.

The Sons of Light versus the Sons of Darkness

Before its discovery by the Bedouin, Qumran Cave 1 sheltered an intriguing scroll that describes a future war between the forces of good and evil. Popularly called the War Scroll, the text opens with this description: "[The Rule of] War on the unleashing of the attack of the sons of light against the company of the sons of darkness, the army of Belial."[2] Here and elsewhere in the War Scroll, the forces of good are called the sons of light (or children of light) and the forces of evil are named the sons of darkness (or children of darkness).

The sons of light will receive divine help from heavenly forces. According to the War Scroll, "the assembly of gods," "Holy Ones" in heaven, and God's angels will assist the sons of light in defeating the forces of evil. One passage reads, "At that time, the assembly of gods and the hosts of men shall battle, causing great carnage; on the day of calamity, the sons of light shall battle with the company of darkness amid the shouts of a mighty multitude and the clamour of gods and men to (make manifest) the might of God."[3] According to another passage, "For the multitude of the Holy Ones [is with Thee] in heaven, and the host of the Angels is in Thy holy abode, praising Thy name. . . . Thou wilt muster the [hosts of] Thine [el]ect, in their Thousands and Myriads, with Thy Holy Ones [and with all] Thine Angels, that they may be mighty in battle, [and may smite] the rebels of the earth by Thy great judgements, and that [they may triumph] together with the elect of heaven."[4]

Yet another passage refers to the "angelic host": "Valiant [warriors] of the angelic host are among our numbered men, and the Hero of war is with our congregation; the host of His spirits is with our foot-soldiers and horsemen. [They are as] clouds, as clouds of dew (covering) the earth, as a shower of rain shedding judgement on all that grows on the earth."[5]

In the end, the sons of light will successfully defeat the sons of darkness: "This shall be a time of salvation for the people of God, an age of dominion for all the members of His company, and of everlasting destruction for all the company of Belial. . . . The dominion of the Kittim shall come to an end and iniquity shall be vanquished, leaving no remnant; [for the sons] of darkness there shall be no escape. [The sons of righteous]ness shall shine over all the ends of the earth; they

The War Scroll describes a future war between the forces of good and evil, or the sons of light and the sons of darkness.

shall go on shining until all the seasons of darkness are consumed and, at the season appointed by God, His exalted greatness shall shine eternally to the peace, blessing, glory, joy, and long life of all the sons of light."[6]

The War Scroll describes the organization of the army of Israel in detail and prescribes prayers, hymns, and exhortations to be spoken by the priests and Levites in the course of war. The prayers and hymns focus on God and his great power, mercies, and marvelous works. The War Scroll refers to God multiple times: God of our fathers, God's marvels, God of mercies, God's battle, just God, people of God, time of God, God's might, the people redeemed by God, and God's great hand. In point of fact, God's role in the war between the sons of light and the sons of darkness will be so prominent that God's people will write expressions on their trumpets and banners that include the name of God: "Rallied by God," "Princes of God," "Peace of God," "Time Appointed by God," plus others.

Ultimately it is God who will give victory to the righteous. The author of the War Scroll cites Moses, "Furthermore, (Moses) taught us, 'Thou art in the midst of us, a mighty God and terrible, causing all our enemies to flee before [us].' . . . Truly the battle is Thine! Their bodies are crushed by the might of Thy hand and there is no man to bury them. . . . Truly the battle is Thine and the power from Thee! It is not ours. Our strength and the power of our hands accomplish no mighty deeds except by Thy power and the might of Thy great valour."[7]

Showing Gratitude to God—the Thanksgiving Hymns

The Thanksgiving Hymns, discovered in Caves 1 and 4, consist of some two dozen hymns. They are similar to a hymnbook (but without the musical notes) and are called Thanksgiving Hymns because of their frequent repetition of the phrase "I thank thee, O Lord." The hymns contain phraseology similar to the biblical psalms; the hymns include praises of God's acts of salvation, his judgments, and his works of creation. The hymns describe the human tendency to sin and the condition in which humankind finds itself. In these hymns—as in many of the psalms—God's righteousness, mercy, and truth are emphasized.

The authorship of the hymns is unknown, although some scholars maintain that one called the Teacher of Righteousness wrote the hymns; others believe that multiple writers authored the hymns.

The following thanksgiving hymn (Hymn 5) is characteristic of other hymns of this genre that are part of the Dead Sea Scrolls:

> [I thank] Thee, O Lord,
> as befits the greatness of Thy
>   power
> and the multitude of Thy marvels
>   for ever and ever.
> [Thou art a merciful God] and rich
>   in [favours],
> pardoning those who repent of
>   their sin
> and visiting the iniquity of the
>   wicked.

Thanksgiving Hymns

The "haves and have-nots"

"[Elisha] Qimron's revelation of this extraordinary scroll [a *Halakhic Letter*] shattered our customary complacency. When we realized that a document so central to the history of the Qumran sect and, indeed, of Second Temple Judaism, had been withheld from the academic community for so long, we were outraged. Qimron's disclosure made us acutely aware of the unfair distribution of texts, of the existence of haves and have-nots among Dead Sea Scrolls scholars."

Lawrence H. Schiffman, *Reclaiming the Dead Sea Scrolls* (Jerusalem: The Jewish Publication Society, 1994), xviii.

[Thou delightest in] the free-will
offering [of the righteous]
but iniquity Thou hatest always.
Thou hast favoured me, Thy servant,
with a spirit of knowledge,
[that I may choose] truth [and
goodness]
and loathe all the ways of iniquity.
And I have loved Thee freely
and with all my heart;
[contemplating the mysteries of]
Thy wisdom
[I have sought Thee].
For this is from Thy hand
and [nothing is done] without [Thy
will].[8]

A Noteworthy Sectarian Document: Some Observances of the Law

Cave 4 yielded six tattered copies of an important legal document that scholars call MMT (from the Hebrew, *Miqsat Ma'ase ha-Torah*), or Some Observances of the Law. MMT, a sectarian document of great importance, is polemical in its approach. Both the author and its audience, or addressee, are unknown. The textual evidence of MMT, when weighed together with other Qumran documents, suggests that its author was the Teacher of Righteousness and its recipient was the Wicked Priest, or perhaps opponents of the Qumran community. Inasmuch as the opening portion of the document no longer exists, scholars do not know its literary classification, but some propose that it was a letter, owing to its content and language.

MMT deals with three central themes: (1) the sacred calendar, touching on items that pertain to the Sabbath, the Festival of Weeks, a Memorial Day, the Festival of the (New) Wine, the Festival of the (New) Oil, the [Wood] Offering, and the 364-day calendar; (2) practices relating to the temple, its sacrifices, and laws regarding purity; and (3) laws that pertain to marriage and intermarriage, especially as they affect the priests. These three themes were also important to other Jewish sects of the period, and MMT provides evidence as to the possible reason the Jews of the Qumran community separated themselves from other sects.

More specifically, MMT sets forth many religious laws and precepts belonging to the Qumran community, including mention of:

- the offering of sacrifices from the Gentiles
- laws regarding the red heifer
- slaughtering outside of the camp
- bringing certain animal skins to the temple
- purity laws regarding the making of vessels from the bones or skins of unclean animals
- Jerusalem as the chosen place
- Jerusalem and its holiness
- sacrificing pregnant animals
- eating unborn animals
- items concerning the blind and the deaf
- prohibition against bringing dogs into Jerusalem
- tithes and fruits given to the priests
- items concerning lepers

The document concludes with the admonishment "Understand all these (matters) and ask Him (God) to straighten your counsel and put you far away from thoughts of evil and the counsel of Belial. Consequently, you will rejoice at the end of time when you discover that some of our sayings are true. And it will be reckoned for you as righteousness when you perform what is right and good before Him, for your own good and for that of Israel."[9]

The Rule of the Community—A Key Document

One of the central, organizational documents found among the Dead Sea Scrolls, one that is unique to the Qumran community, is the Rule of the Community, a designation that is found in the text itself. The Rule of the Community, which dates to about 100 BC, is sometimes called the Manual of Discipline since the document includes regulations and directives regarding how the Jews who owned the scrolls should live. The number of (fragmented) copies of the Rule of the Community discovered at Qumran—ten in Cave 4 and one in Cave 5—indicates that this was an important document to the Jews who owned it. The Rule of the Community (1QS) consists of six sections:

1. Introduction (I, 1–15)
2. Instructions regarding the ritual for those who enter into the covenant or who renew the covenant annually (I, 16–III, 12)
3. An explanation of many of the beliefs of the community, especially some of the dualistic doctrines regarding two opposing spirits, one of truth and the other of injustice (III, 13–IV, 26)
4. Various rules and directives for members of the community (V, 1–VII, 25), including a list of penalties (ranging from loss of rations to expulsion from the community) for various types of infractions, suggesting something of the strictness of the group. The list of penalties instructs that:

Whoever has deliberately lied shall do penance for six months.

Whoever has deliberately insulted his companion unjustly shall do penance for one year and shall be excluded.

Whoever has deliberately deceived his companion by word or by deed shall do penance for six months. . . .

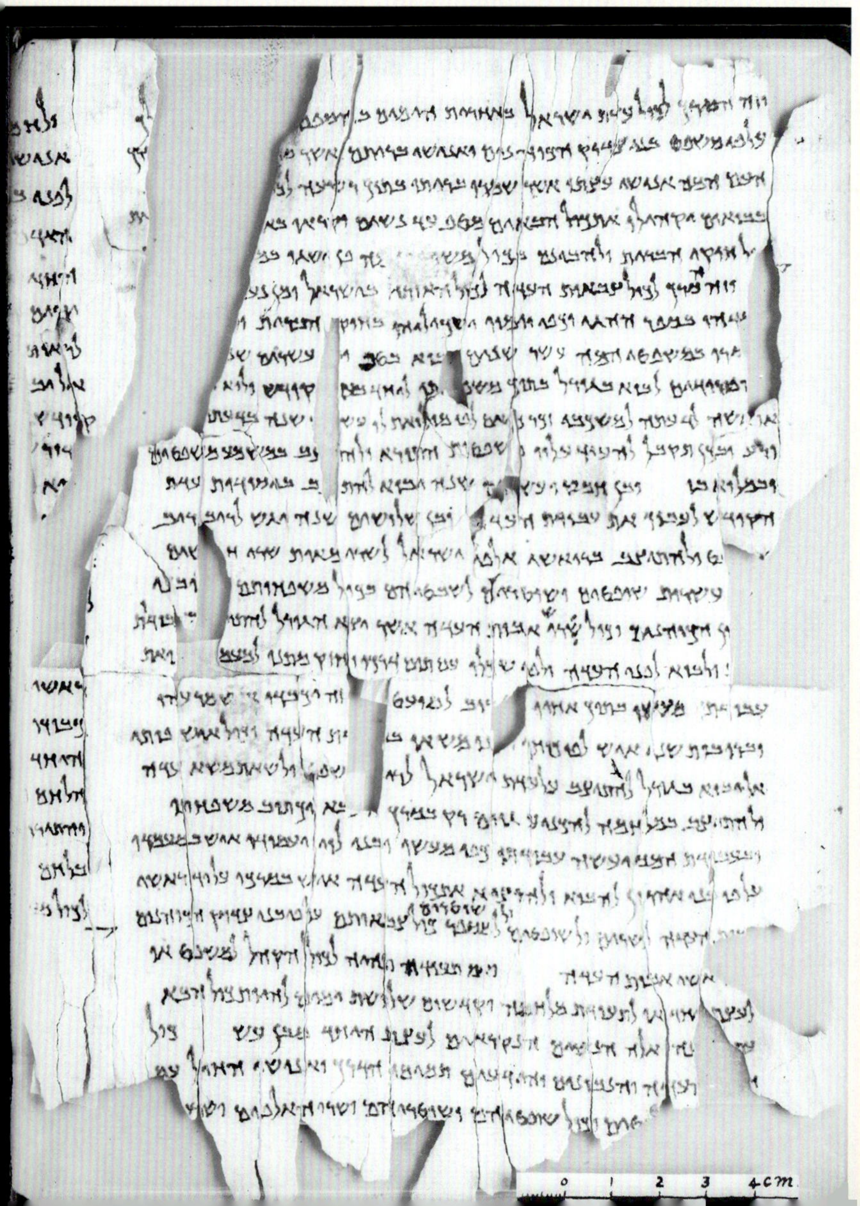

The Rule of the Community sets forth rules and regulations regarding how the Jews who owned the scrolls should live.

Whoever has borne malice against his companion unjustly shall do penance for six months/one year; and likewise, whoever has taken revenge in any matter whatever.

Whoever has spoken foolishly: three months.

Whoever has interrupted his companion whilst speaking: ten days.

Whoever has lain down to sleep during an Assembly of the Congregation: thirty days. And likewise, whoever has left, without reason, an Assembly of the Congregation as many as three times during one Assembly, shall do penance for ten days. But if he has departed whilst they were standing he shall do penance for thirty days.[10]

5. This section (VIII, 1–X, 8), which seems to represent the heart of the Rule of the Community, sets forth various rules regarding the conduct of community members as they study God's laws and "prepare the way of God." It also describes the leader's duties and contains items pertaining to the liturgical calendar.

6. The final section sets forth a hymn (X, 9–XI, 22).

This document was designed for a faithful "remnant" of Israel who was preparing the "way in the desert" for the kingdom of God and for God's triumph over the forces of evil. This document contains a preamble explaining the community's purpose, its basic constitution (including the requirements for entrance into the community), the various classes or ranks within the community, the regulations governing the relations among the members of the community, items concerning military service, education, eligibility for office, and the conduct of communal meals.

The Rule of the Community also contains the following basic steps in the initiation process: an expression of willingness to enter the covenant, collective confession of wrongdoing and acknowledgment of God's mercy, and blessing those who enter into the covenant.

In many respects, explains Geza Vermes, the Rule of the Community parallels community regulations for later Christian groups in their documents known as the *Didache*, the *Apostolic Constitutions*, the *Didascalia*, and the *Rule of Benedict*. These documents are all products of the early Christian centuries and, like the Rule of the Community, are concerned with providing a constitution for their communities as well as a pattern for daily living.

The New Jerusalem Texts

Several fragmented Aramaic documents provide details regarding the New Jerusalem that will exist near the end of times. The documents likely formed a significant part of the Qumran library, as they were discovered in Caves 1, 2, 4, 5, and 11. The texts describe a visionary or prophet led by a heavenly ministrant who shows him the dimensions of various parts of the New Jerusalem and its temple. The angel first shows the prophet the city, including its twelve gates (each named after the twelve patriarchs, for example, Simeon, Joseph, Reuben, Naphtali, and Asher), towers, large streets, and blocks of houses. Part of one of the fragments from Cave 4 reads, "[And they] c[al]l [the name of] this (one)

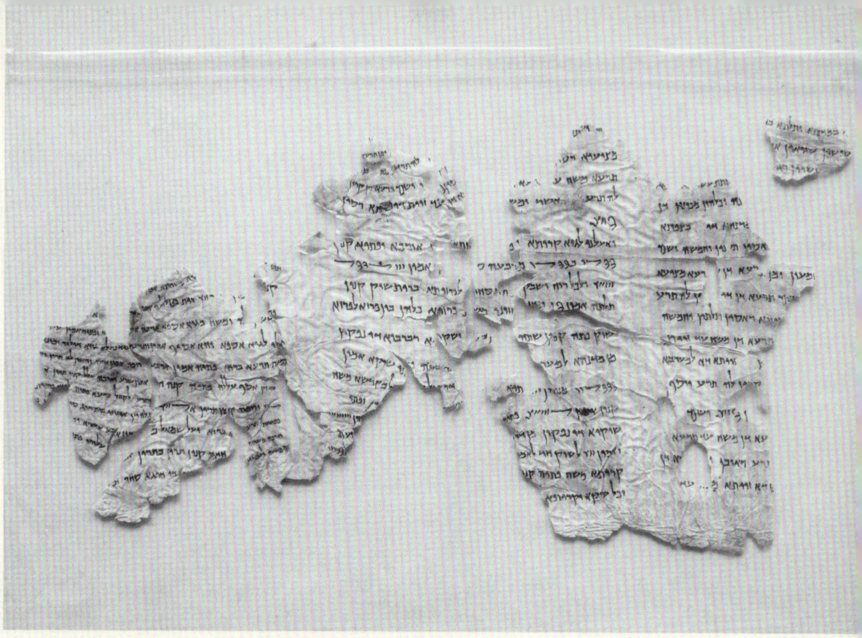

A description of the New Jerusalem (from Cave 4) written in Aramaic. This scroll refers to the temple and the magnificence of the New Jerusalem.

[Gate] of Naphtali. And from this gate he measured to the [eastern] gate 25 [s]tadia. And they call this gate Gate of Asher. And he measu[red from] this [ga]te to the eastern corner 25 stadia. *vacat* And he led me into the city, and he measured each block of houses for its length and width, fifty-one reeds by fifty-one, in a square."[11]

Building materials for this new city, apparently, will be of very high quality. For example, one line states: "And all [the streets of the city] are paved with white stone . . . marble and jasper."[12]

Then the angel shows him the temple's exterior and interior. Although the New Jerusalem texts are fragmented, they seem to refer to the temple's architectural measurements and materials, courtyard, utensils, priestly vestments, altar, sacrificial animals, religious festivals, and throne. New Jerusalem also describes the temple's rituals and ceremonies, such as the distribution of the offerings and the shewbread.

The documents seem to position the New Jerusalem in the context of the end of days.

The literary form of the New Jerusalem texts brings to mind Ezekiel 40–46, where Ezekiel was hosted by an angel who revealed to him the future Jerusalem temple and its dimensions. The angel's part in both visions—Ezekiel's and that of the New Jerusalem texts—was not passive or secondary; he had an active role. The angel in Ezekiel escorted the prophet from place to place in and around the future temple. On twenty-six occasions Ezekiel wrote that the angel "brought me," "he brought me," or "brought he me" from one place to the next. For example, "then brought he me into the outward court" (Ezekiel 40:17); "and he brought me to the inner court" (Ezekiel 40:28), and so forth. Similar language is found in the New Jerusalem texts.

Ancient Scriptural Commentaries

The Jews who owned the scrolls wrote out their interpretations of several scriptural passages from the Old Testament books of Isaiah, Habakkuk, Hosea, Micah, Nahum, and Psalms. These commentaries reveal a striking method of biblical interpretation that generally consists of three components: (1) the citation of a passage of scripture; (2) a formula that introduces the explanation, which usually uses the words "its interpretation" or "interpreted"; and (3) likening the scriptural passage to themselves (that is, the Qumran community of believers) by arguing that its fulfillment had reference either to themselves or to contemporary events.

Most of the commentaries are severely fragmented because of the harshness of the elements over time, although substantial portions of both Pesher Habakkuk and Pesher Psalms[a] exist today. The two most popular biblical books, in terms of the number of commentaries about them discovered in the Qumran caves, are Isaiah (six commentaries) and Psalms (three commentaries). The following is an example from the commentary on Psalm 37. The passage in italics represents the verse from Psalm 37, which is followed by the interpretation in regular font:

> *[Be sil]ent before [the Lord and] long for him, and be not heated against the successful, the man who [achi]eves his plans.* (Psalm 37:7)
>
> Its interpretation concerns the Liar who has led astray many by his lying words so that they chose frivolous things and heeded not the interpreter of knowledge . . . they shall perish by the sword and famine and plague.
>
> *Relent from anger and abandon wrath. Do not be angry; it tends only to evil for the wicked shall be cut off.* (Psalm 37:8–9)
>
> Interpreted, this concerns all those who return to the Law, to those who do not refuse to turn away from their evil. For all those who are stubborn in turning away from their iniquity shall be cut off.
>
> *But those who wait for the Lord shall possess the land.* (Psalm 37:9)
>
> Interpreted, this is the congregation of His elect who do His will.
>
> *A little while and the wicked shall be no more; I will look towards his place but he shall not be there.* (Psalm 37:10)

Interpreted, this concerns all the wicked. At the end of the forty years they shall be blotted out and no [evil] man shall be found on the earth.

But the humble shall possess the land and delight in abundant peace. (Psalm 37:11)

Interpreted, this concerns [the congregation of the] Poor who shall accept the season of penance and shall be delivered from all the snares of Belial. Afterwards, all who possess the earth shall delight and prosper on exquisite food.

The commentary continues in the same manner—presentation of a passage of scripture followed by an interpretation. Notice how the author of the commentary likens the scriptures to his own time and his own community. Such an approach of likening the scriptures to the present community of believers is also a practice in our era. Similar commentaries, authored by theological authorities or scholars, find a place in the modern world in numerous faiths and religions.

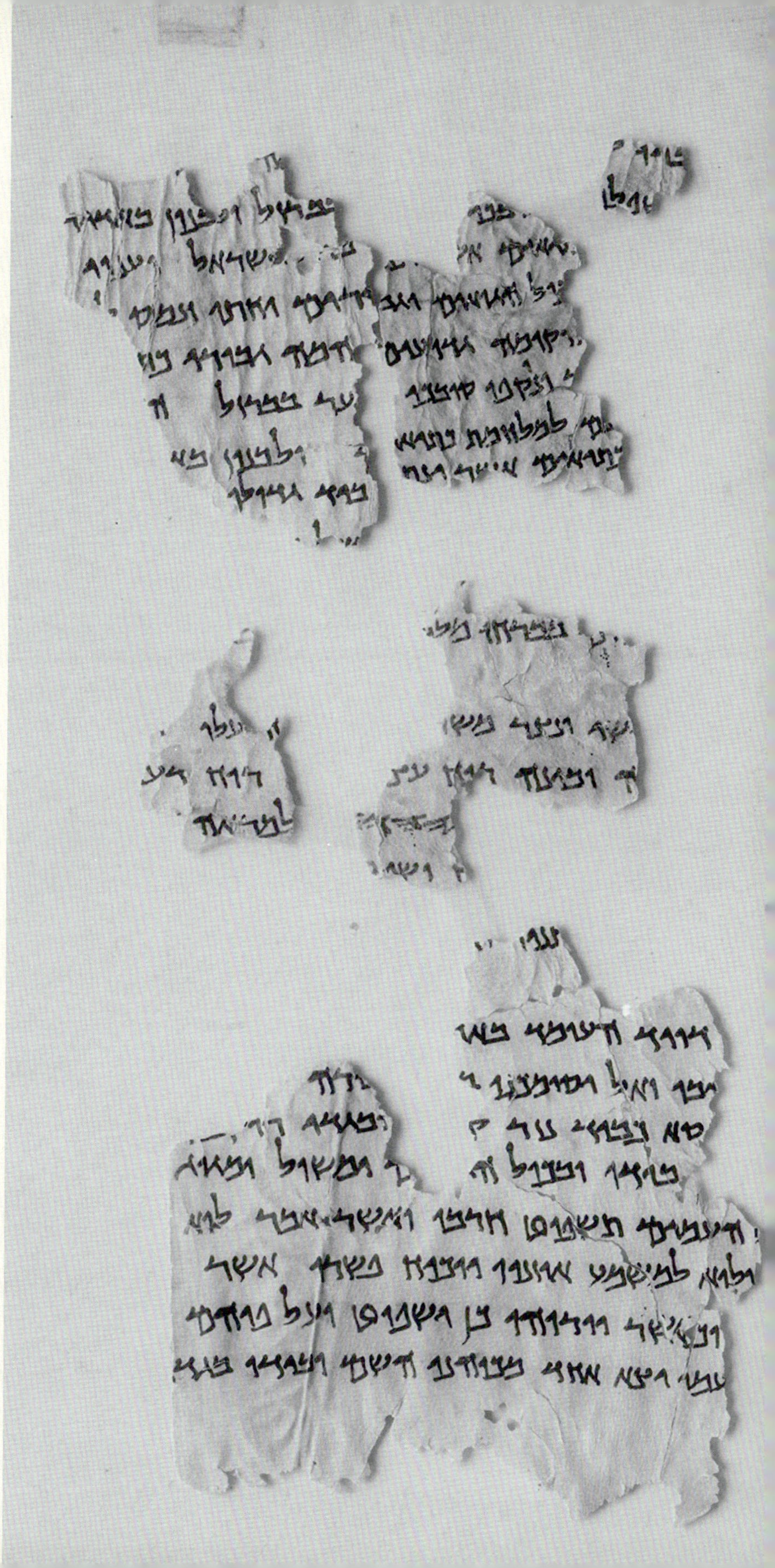

Isaiah's writings were of such great value to those who inhabited Qumran that they authored commentaries on Isaiah. The fragments in the photo to the right are a commentary of Isaiah from Cave 4.

Treasure Scrolls, Puzzles, and Mysteries

A Cipher or Secret Code—Text Written Backwards

Certain scrolls present unsolved puzzles and enigmas. For example, one scroll comprises cryptic texts, or texts that are written in code. Another is a composition written on a copper scroll that details the whereabouts of massive hidden treasures of gold, silver, spices, and precious objects—treasures that presumably once belonged to Herod's temple. Yet another scroll oddly features some words written in red ink rather than in the standard black ink. Other scrolls present the name Jehovah with four dots or in an ancient form of Hebrew, possibly to protect against improper utterance of this sacred name.

The scrolls also present many questions that have perplexed scholars since their discovery in 1947. Did Jesus Christ at one time live among the Jews who owned the scrolls? Was he their Teacher of Righteousness? Did John the Baptist dwell and study with the scrolls' owners? Did that group of Jews have a bible that consisted of numerous other books beyond those belonging to our present Old Testament? That is to say, were the Temple Scroll, Reworked Pentateuch, Enoch, Noah, Beatitudes, and other scrolls part of their authorized canon of scripture? And do these texts hold religious authority or significance for Judaism, Christianity, and other religions of today? All of these items, and many more, comprise puzzles and mysteries of the scrolls.

One text from Cave 4 presents a mysterious text that is written backwards, probably to conceal the text's meaning to the casual reader. This text is unparalleled among the Dead Sea Scrolls; Hebrew is normally written from right to left, but this text is written from left to right. For this reason, Vermes calls it a "childish cipher."[1] Scholars have named this text 4QHoroscope (4Q186) because it appears to be an ancient horoscope, although we cannot identify the text with certainty because of its fragmented nature.

To demonstrate what a text written backwards looks like, I have provided an excerpt of 4QHoroscope, using the English translation:

> ni (strap) xis fo stsisnoc tirips siH eht ni eerht dna thgiL fo esuoH eht stsisnoc tirips siH . . . ssenkrad fo tiP fo esuoH eht ni (strap) thgie fo fo esuoH eht morf eno dna ssenkraD thgie fo stsisnoc tirips siH . . . thgiL . . . thgiL fo esuoH eht ni] (strap) .[ssenkraD fo esuoH eht ni] eno dna

The Copper Scroll (*left*), as discovered in Qumran Cave 3, is a treasure map of sorts.

A "real buried treasure"

"Almost all scholars today believe the Copper Scroll describes real buried treasure, contrary to the view of Milik and the official scroll team."

Hershel Shanks, *The Copper Scroll and the Search for the Temple Treasure* (Washington, DC: Biblical Archaeology Society, 2007), 41.

Now, reading the text in normal English (left to right), the same excerpt reads as follows:

> His spirit consists of six (parts) in the House of Light and three in the Pit of darkness . . . His spirit consists of eight (parts) in the House of Darkness and one from the House of Light . . . His spirit consists of eight (parts) [in the House of Light . . . and one [in the House of Darkness].

Vermes briefly explains the meaning of this passage: "The spiritual qualities of three individuals described in the work are reflected in their share of Light and Darkness. The first man is very wicked: eight parts of Darkness to a single part of Light. The second man is largely good: six parts of Light against three parts of Darkness. The last is almost perfect: eight portions of Light and only one of Darkness."[2] 4QHoroscope also provides physical descriptions of the three men according to their degree of virtue or wickedness. For example, the third man who is almost perfect has a gentle voice, fine teeth, glowing eyes, smooth thighs, and well-aligned toes. In contrast, the text describes the man who is eight parts of darkness: "His teeth are of uneven length (?). His fingers are thick, and his thighs are thick and very hairy, each one. His toes are thick and short."[3]

A Treasure Scroll Worthy of Indiana Jones

Among the most puzzling of the scrolls is the Copper Scroll, which is extraordinary for several reasons: its unique Hebrew orthography (method of spelling), its use of a Hebrew script and dialect that are unlike that of other scrolls, its use of metal as a means of textual transmission, and its contents regarding deposits of treasures. The Copper Scroll is a treasure map of sorts. This last item—the inscription of the location of treasures—has fascinated treasure seekers since the scroll's discovery in the early 1950s. Both textual scholars and archaeologists have exerted great efforts to locate the treasures described in this scroll, but with no success.

The Copper Scroll, discovered in Qumran Cave 3, was formed from a single plaque of copper-based metal that was fairly well preserved because of its metal content. On this was inscribed, in twelve columns of text, a list of sixty-four deposits of gold, silver, aromatic spices, sacred vestments, and manuscripts. Because of the enormous amount of treasure involved—perhaps as much as several tons—many are convinced that the treasures described in the document are fictional. Others, including a large group of bona fide scholars, have argued that the scroll records the deposition of the massive treasures of the Jerusalem temple, perhaps tithes and offerings collected during the First Jewish Revolt that could not be taken to Jerusalem during the siege.

The Copper Scroll begins with these words:

> A Horebbah which is in the Vale of Achor under the stairs which go eastwards forty cubits: a box (filled with) silver weighing in all seventeen talents. **KEN**. In the tomb of . . . the third: 100 gold bars. In the great cistern which is in the courtyard of the little colonnade, at its very bottom, closed with sediment towards the upper opening: nine hundred

talents. At the hill of Kohlit, containers, sandalwood and ephods (priestly garments).[4]

After these opening words, the scroll continues with descriptions of sixty-four deposits of hidden treasures. Several mysteries remain: what is the meaning of the Greek and unidentifiable characters that are located throughout the Copper Scroll, including the following: **KEN**, **HN**, **E**, **I**, **XA**? Are these codes designed to unravel the puzzle of the location of the treasures? If so, what do they signify? Another mystery pertains to the fact that the geographical markers described on the scroll (Horebbah, great cistern, hill of Kohlit, exit of the canal, and others) are unknown today. Perhaps the unidentifiable Greek characters and the unknown geographical markers have made it difficult, if not impossible, for archaeologists and treasure seekers to locate the treasures. Whoever breaks the code of the Copper Scroll will become famous, and perhaps very wealthy.

Qumran Cave 3 contained the Copper Scroll.

A specialist carefully sawed the extremely fragile Copper Scroll into strips to enable scholars to research and translate it.

Safeguarding the Divine Name Jehovah

The name Jehovah (most English translations of the Bible supply Lord where the name Jehovah appears) was one of the most sacred of deific names to the Jews who owned the scrolls. The Qumran writers and scribes often presented the name Jehovah in very unique ways, for they employed various surrogates when writing it (that is, the Hebrew equivalent) on the scrolls. For example, they used four dots (that is, ····) instead of the name Jehovah in a number

A segment from the Copper Scroll shows a close-up view of the Hebrew characters. This scroll consists of a list of sixty-four deposits of treasures.

Sharing the scrolls with other scholars

"In 1987, at a public session of a Scrolls Symposium held in London, I urged [John Strugnell] to publish at once the photographic plates, while he and his acolytes carried on their work at their customary snail's pace. This request was met with a one-syllable answer: no."

Geza Vermes, *An Introduction to the Complete Dead Sea Scrolls* (Minneapolis, MN: Fortress Press, 1999), 7.

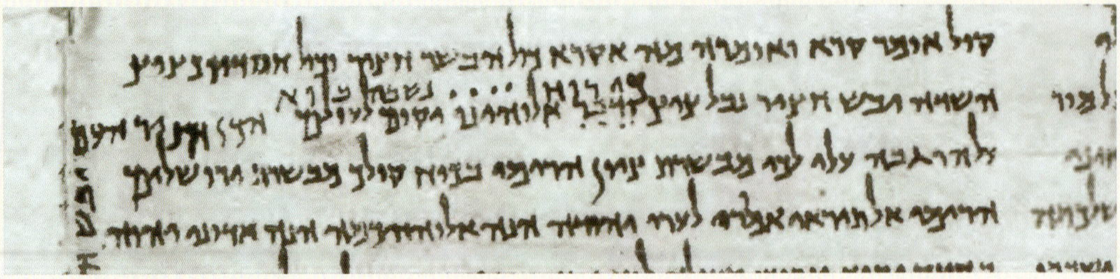

In the Great Isaiah Scroll, a scribe wrote the Divine Name Jehovah with four dots (between lines 1 and 2) to differentiate it from other words.

of compositions (see 1QIsa^a Isaiah 40:7; 1QS, 4Q175, 4Q176, and others). To illustrate the idea of four dots with an English translation, I present Isaiah 40:3: "Prepare ye the way of · · · · , make straight in the desert a highway for our God."

In addition to using four dots to designate Jehovah, the Dead Sea Scrolls writers also used strange or esoteric Hebrew characters as replacements for Jehovah (see, for example, 4Q266 and 1QS VIII, 13), or they placed this divine name in paleo-Hebrew characters (a very ancient form of Hebrew), rather than in the typical square (Jewish) Hebrew script (see, for example, 1QpHab, 4Q161, 4Q171, 4Q183). This would be akin to our printing the name/title Lord in a different font, as in the following illustration: "Prepare ye the way of the LORD, make straight in the desert a highway for our God."

Why did the Qumran writers use substitutes for this divine name? Scholars have theorized multiple reasons: They did so apparently to set it apart from common words in order to remind the reader of its sanctity; to protect it from erasure because a Jewish directive prevented the scribes from erasing God's name from a writing material; or to prompt a reader lest he accidentally pronounce it while reading the text (the Jews generally used substitute sacred names, such as Adonai, when reading texts out loud).

Moses Segal summarizes the prevailing view of scholars concerning the avoidance of this divine name when he argues that during the postexilic period "a heightened sense of the sanctity of Deity and of the sacredness of its own proper name led to the avoidance of a too frequent employment of the name YHWH (Jehovah) which gradually became ineffable, and to its replacement by a synonymous substitute."[5]

Scroll Conspiracies

Since the Dead Sea Scrolls were discovered between the years 1947 and 1956, it has taken more than fifty years to translate and publish them in legitimate scholarly publications. This time span has encouraged some to ask why it has taken so long to publish the scrolls and if there has been a conspiracy. Some individuals have claimed that the Vatican, the Great Rabbinate, the Council of Churches, or certain authorities suppressed the publication of the scrolls because of the fear that the scrolls had the potential to undermine the faith of Christians or Jews. The idea of scroll conspiracies is ever popular because many people are captivated by such plots and intrigues.

Florentino García-Martínez describes two versions of this myth that have prevailed for many years:

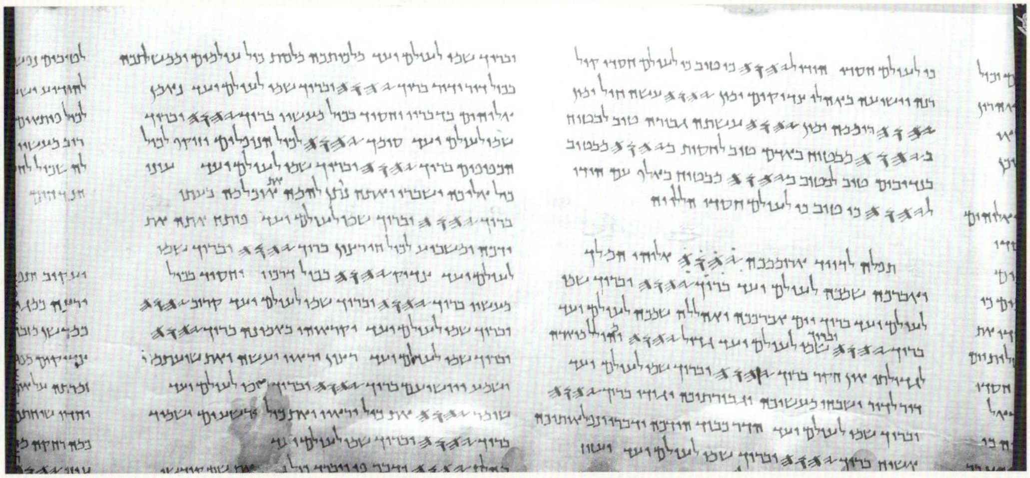

To set the Divine Name Jehovah apart from other words, a scribe wrote it in paleo-Hebrew characters (a very ancient form of Hebrew) in Psalm 145, rather than using the typical square (Jewish) Hebrew script (see the Divine Name in paleo-Hebrew, middle of line 2, left column).

The content of this myth in its crudest form can be expressed as follows. Among the Dead Sea Scrolls there are many texts the publication of which would pose a great danger for the established religions, Judaism as well as Christianity. These alleged texts would allow the falsehood of both Christianity and Judaism as a religion to be demonstrated. For this reason, the religious authorities (Jewish and Christian alike) have prevented their publication until now. In another version of the myth, the religious authorities (the Great Rabbinate, the Vatican or the Council of Churches) are not involved. Instead, the actual research scholars responsible for publication (some of whom are priests or ministers) willingly censored certain texts which offended their religious sensibilities or delayed their publication to prevent the harm they could do to the faithful.[6]

Such claims are mythical and are built upon sensationalism or misinformation. Valid explanations for the delay in publication of the scrolls are many and varied.

Lack of scholarly access

Most scholars generally were not permitted access to the scrolls until the early 1990s, at which time the pace of translating and publishing the scrolls increased.

Limited access to the scrolls

The majority of the scholars assigned to translate the scrolls were professors who lived far away from Jerusalem, where most of the scrolls are stored. Because of their teaching assignments and because of the great distance they had to travel to study the actual scrolls, most scholars had limited access to them.

An enormous task

The great number of manuscripts and fragments, combined with their poor condition, created a task of gigantic proportions, including the identification and piecing together of thousands of small scroll fragments. The work of translating the scrolls was underestimated by the

"The scrollery clique"

"I am starting a campaign, very quietly for the moment, to get the scrollery clique broken up and new blood injected, with the idea of getting some of that stuff Milik, Strugnell, and Starky are sitting on published quickly in provisional form. . . . Please say nothing to anybody for the moment—it's a ticklish situation. But you will agree that something must be done, and that soon."

John Allegro to Pro. Muilenburg, Oct 31, 1957. Judith Anne Brown, *John Marco Allegro: The Maverick of the Dead Sea Scrolls* (Grand Rapids, MI: Eerdmans, 2005), 158–59.

original seven members of the translation team—it was a matter of too much being expected of too few.

Lack of proper funding
Dead Sea Scrolls translators and scholars often lacked proper financial support to carry on their work. They often were required to finance their own work and travel to Jerusalem, often with an extended stay in that city. Such economic challenges created hardships and delayed the publication of the scrolls.

Sensationalistic Claims about the Scrolls

Since their discovery, the scrolls have attracted much notice; both scholars and laypersons have turned their attention to them. The popular press has unveiled the scrolls to the public, but often with misinformed and sensationalistic approaches. Even several established printing houses, newspapers, news magazines, and quarterlies have published irresponsible content about the scrolls. The content and presentation of tabloids are by far the worst because they make various sensationalistic but unsubstantiated claims. Some tantalizing headlines follow:

> "Dead Sea Scrolls Predict 2009 Flood"
>
> "Dead Sea Scrolls HUGE Cover Up!"
>
> "Is Jesus in the Dead Sea Scrolls?"

Some irresponsible assertions about the Dead Sea Scrolls include claims that (1) the scrolls predict a flood in 2009 of biblical proportions that would cause more than two billion persons to drown (a claim that obviously did not come to pass); (2) aliens from outer space have visited the earth; (3) the scrolls provide a cure for AIDS; (4) the scrolls provide predictions of the future, including the date of the world's end; and (5) the scrolls refer to UFOs, including one that would crash in Washington, DC.

Additionally, some writers declare that the scrolls refer to Jesus Christ or his disciples, that the Three Wise Men provided Jesus with "cosmic consciousness," that Jesus married a woman some time after his crucifixion, that the scrolls predict the date of Jesus's second coming, and that the apostle Paul served as a spy for the Roman government.

The various sensationalistic claims that have been published over the years share common points:

- They lack proper textual support from the Dead Sea Scrolls for their claims. In other words, those writing the claims do not reveal which scrolls actually provide a cure for AIDS or which scrolls explain that the apostle Paul was a spy.
- They lack responsible bibliographic references.
- The authors who write and publish these claims are not mainstream scholars in the field of Qumran studies; usually they are not scholars at all.
- They are sensational to the point that the claims are shocking or scandalous.

Happily, one does not need such sensationalism because the scrolls, on their own, are astounding and spectacular.

Red-Ink Passages

Soot from oil lamps provided material for manufacturing the ink used on the scrolls.

Scribes consistently used a carbon-based ink, often prepared from the soot of oil lamps, when they wrote the words on leather or papyrus. Although black ink was the standard color, a scribe used red ink for single words and short phrases in a number of passages in one copy of the book of Numbers (4QNum^{b}; see also Numbers 20:22–23; 22:21). Other scribes utilized red ink in specific passages in Psalm 103 and in two nonbiblical scrolls (4Q270 and 4Q481D). The use of red ink in a few scattered passages in a few scrolls is perplexing. Scholars theorize that the red ink marks a passage to be read or perhaps emphasized in the synagogue or in another liturgical setting. But if this were the case, why weren't other well-known liturgical passages also written in red? The red ink remains a mystery.

The scrolls and controversy

"In March 1990 I got a rapid introduction to how controversial the scrolls had become. When asked by a newspaper reporter whether I would be willing to show the photographs to others, I said yes. That one short answer soon had others on the telephone, and my comment was published and reported in several places. Willingness to show others the photographs was a departure from official policy, so it seems. It was even termed a major breakthrough! I still cannot understand why anyone should deny others the right to examine the pictures of scroll fragments, but the experience illustrated the tensions and strong feelings then surrounding the whole issue of access to the scrolls. As I have learned more about what happened in the nearly forty years of scholarship on the Cave 4 manuscripts, I began to understand more about the genesis of people's feelings on both sides of the issue."

James C. VanderKam, *The Dead Sea Scrolls Today* (Grand Rapids, MI: Eerdmans, 1994), xi–xii.

Mysterious Scribal Marks

Scrolls scholar Emanuel Tov has identified and named about seventy-nine different scribal signs or marks that appear in the margins or between the lines of texts of both biblical and nonbiblical scrolls. To the modern eye, each of these marks looks exotic and perhaps mysterious.

Many of these handwritten signs possess identifiable meanings or interpretations; for instance, some scribal signs are section markers or paragraphing symbols (sort of like our paragraphs, chapters, or verses), while others point to corrections in the readings. Still others serve as numbering devices, omission or insertion symbols, parentheses, dots indicating the redivision of words, or cancellation dots.

Although Tov has ascertained the meaning of many of the marks, other marks are esoteric or cryptic, and their meanings remain mystifying to the modern-day reader. For instance, the Isaiah scroll includes *X*-shaped scribal marks, a hat-shaped symbol, a *Z*-shaped symbol, a circular symbol, and other scribal marks. Dead Sea Scrolls scholars and others will continue to puzzle over these mysterious marks and attempt to elucidate their meaning.[7]

Two scribal marks are visible in a margin of the Great Isaiah Scroll: a character that looks like an X near the top and another character that has the appearance of a hat at the bottom.

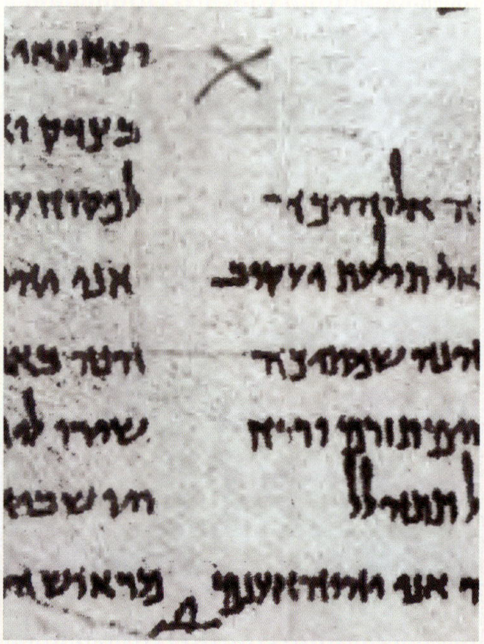

A Giant Jigsaw Puzzle

Most of the scrolls are fragmented, consisting of thousands (some estimate 15,000) of pieces of leather or papyrus in various sizes and shapes. Soon after the discovery of the scrolls, scholars began the process of sorting through the fragments, attempting to reassemble them into scrolls. Doing so, however, was similar to piecing together a huge jigsaw puzzle but with thousands of the pieces missing and without the benefit of a colorful box cover depicting the full picture of the puzzle. Because of the enormous challenge of sorting and piecing the fragments together, scholars developed several approaches to determine which fragments belonged to a specific text.

Types of writing materials

The fragments were sorted into groups of leather parchment or papyri. The scholars continued the sorting process by evaluating the thickness and color of the leather of each fragment.

Scribal handwriting styles

Each of the scribes who copied the texts possessed a unique handwriting style, just as individuals today have singular approaches to handwriting. Paleographers study the book hand (the cursive, shape, and size of characters) and are able to identify different scribes' styles and cursive and, to some extent, to determine which fragments belong together.

Horizontal and vertical lines
For a brief discussion on rulings, see above in the section "What Did the Bible Look Like at the Time of Jesus Christ?"

Scribal markings
Some scribes placed unique markings in the margins of the leather or between the lines of the text. Such scribal markings provide additional clues as scholars sort the fragments.

Familiar expressions
The actual words, if they belong to a previously known text (for example, Genesis, Exodus), are helpful in determining placement of fragments. For instance, when scholars read "every tree of the garden" on a fragment, they recognize that these words likely originate from Genesis 2:15. This fragment, therefore, may belong to the book of Genesis.

Material join
When two fragments have complementing edges (like two pieces of a jigsaw puzzle that belong together), they may fit together.

A divided word
When one fragment has a portion of a word (such as *Melchi*) and another has the other portion (such as *zedek*), scholars can then join the fragments together (to read *Melchizedek*).

The sorting process is a painstaking and tedious task; joining a single fragment to another may take hours or days. Notwithstanding the work involved, joining one fragment with another provides great satisfaction to the scholar.

Piecing together thousands of small scroll fragments signified a task of enormous dimensions. The photo shows thousands of fragments on tables in the Rockefeller Museum.

A huge jigsaw puzzle

"When the thousands of fragments from Cave 4 were brought to the scrollery of the Palestine Archaeological Museum, many of them had to be bought from the Bedouins, who had originally discovered the cave and had begun to clean it out. An effort was thus made by the Jordanian Department of Antiquities to buy all the fragments from the Bedouins because it was realized that only so would it be possible to work on the giant jigsaw puzzle that those fragments would create."

Joseph A. Fitzmyer, *Responses to 101 Questions on the Dead Sea Scrolls* (New York: Paulist Press, 1992), 7.

Modern Technology and the Scrolls

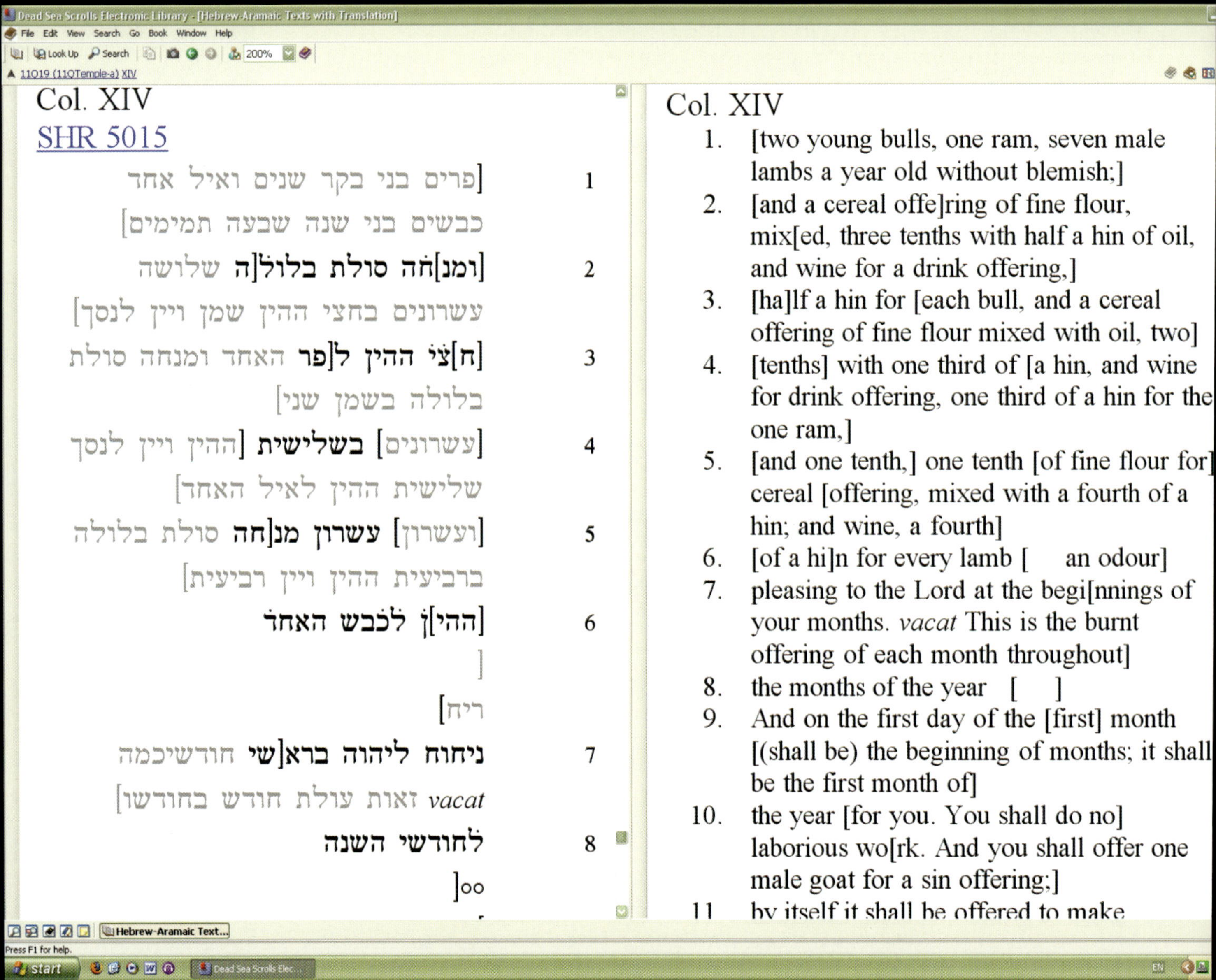

Dating the Scrolls—Modern Science Meets Antiquity

How old are the scrolls? Based on four scientific methods, scholars generally agree that the scrolls were written or copied between the years 250 BC and AD 70.

1. *Paleography*. This refers to the study of ancient writing styles and methods, or the science of deciphering ancient writing systems. After a careful examination of the way the ancient copyists and scribes wrote Hebrew characters on the scrolls, Professor Frank Moore Cross of Harvard University dated the scrolls to three time periods: the Archaic period (250–150 BC), the Hasmonean period (150–30 BC) and the Herodian period (30 BC–AD 68/70).[1]

2. *Accelerator Mass Spectrometry (AMS)*. This method of dating the scrolls is similar to the carbon-14 dating system. Of the eight scrolls tested by AMS, seven of them agree generally with the paleographic dating of the same scrolls.[2]

3. *Artifacts, Pottery, and Coins*. Archaeologists' discoveries of dated coins, pottery or pieces of pottery, and other artifacts may be helpful in dating the scrolls, particularly if such physical remains were located in the same vicinity as the scrolls. Pottery, for example, can often be dated to a specific time frame, and together with coins, such archaeological evidence aids scholars in dating the scrolls.

4. *Internal Historical References*. On rare occasions, the scrolls themselves allude to historical events or characters that assist in dating the scrolls. For example, if a scroll refers to King Herod the Great, who ruled 37–4 BC, scholars would date that scroll during or after Herod's reign, but certainly not before.

This screen shot from *The Dead Sea Scrolls Electronic Reference Library* exhibits Hebrew transcriptions of the Temple Scroll on the left and a translation of the same on the right.

Digitizing the Scrolls, CDs, and More

Perhaps the ancient community of Jews who owned the Dead Sea Scrolls would be astounded to know that digitized

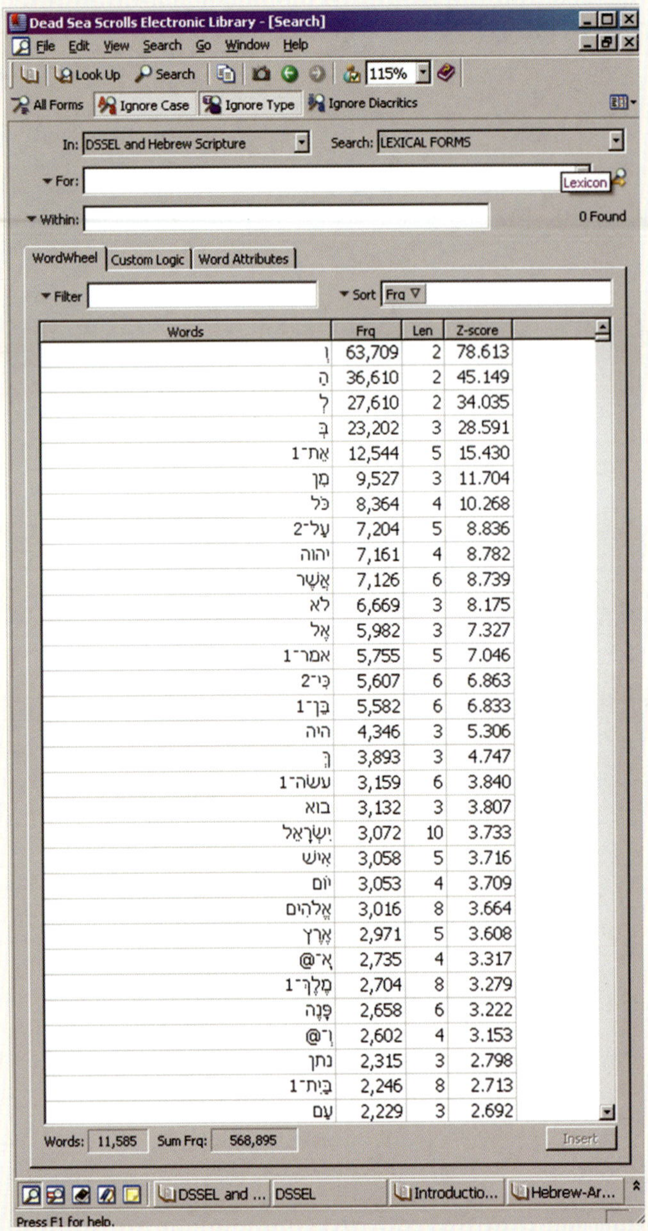

photographic images of all their scrolls (900+ documents) had been placed on a small, round plastic disk called a CD (compact disc).[3] And what would the ancients think of the following?

- The CD is portable—it can be easily carried in one's pocket, anywhere in the world.
- The CD is convenient—one can carry the entire Qumran library in the palm of the hand.
- The CD may be distributed at a relatively low cost to individuals or institutions.
- CD users can study the scrolls without worrying about mishandling the actual scrolls.
- There is no limit to distribution of the CD; literally thousands of individuals may obtain a copy.

Furthermore, in addition to photographic images, this same CD also con-

The *Dead Sea Scrolls Electronic Reference Library* has multiple functions, including the ability to list all the words in order of frequency (the screen shot shows the top 31 words in order of their frequency).

Archaeologists' tools

"The only tools it was possible to use in the clearance of the cave were penknives, brushes, tweezers, and fingers, for the fragments are brittle and easily damaged, and sieving was not possible because of the presence of the stones in the fill."

G. Lankester Harding, "Introductory," in DJD I, 7.

tains transcriptional texts and reference materials of importance for scholarly work on the scrolls—the Hebrew Bible, an English translation of the Hebrew Bible, a dictionary of biblical and Qumran Hebrew, and the Septuagint (Greek translation of the Bible). In addition, the CD includes functions that enable scholars to study the scrolls in ways not possible through other means: complex, instantaneous, comprehensive searches of the transcriptional texts; an exhaustive concordance; the ability to print or store the search results; and the ability to manipulate (flip, rotate, or cut and paste) or zoom in on the images to 500 percent their actual size. This state-of-the-art technology enables individuals to examine the scrolls in new ways that were not possible until recently.

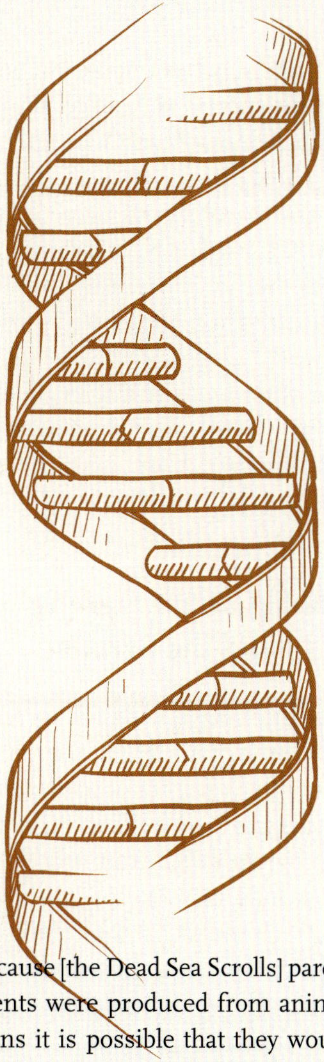

Applying DNA to the Scrolls

Modern-day movies and television programming have popularized DNA analyses in various investigative settings such as crime scenes, courtroom dramatizations, and discovering family roots. Beyond the movie industry, DNA analyses have served a variety of significant purposes for the betterment of society. DNA scientists have also used this branch of knowledge to analyze ancient things—such as leather and bones, teeth, and skin from Egyptian mummies.

DNA scientists have also applied their technology and expertise to analyze the Dead Sea Scrolls. During the mid-1990s, a team of scientists began testing the DNA of a limited number of scrolls and fragments. One such scientist explains how DNA analysis works on the scrolls:

> Because [the Dead Sea Scrolls] parchments were produced from animal skins it is possible that they would contain remnant DNA molecules. Within the last decade new techniques in molecular biology have been developed that have made it possible to recover DNA from ancient sources. The molecular analysis of ancient DNA (aDNA) from the Judean desert parchment fragments would enable us to establish a genetic signature unique for each manuscript. The precision of the DNA analysis will allow us to identify at least three levels of hierarchy: the species, population, and individual animal from which the parchment was produced.[4]

DNA analysis has enabled scholars to identify the species used to create a few of the parchments—at least two parchments were created from either an ibex or gazelle; other parchments came from wild or domestic goats. DNA analysis can also assist scholars in determining whether the library of scrolls came from the immediate region of Qumran and the Dead Sea or from other areas of ancient Palestine. Additionally, DNA analysis could facilitate piecing together those small fragments that are presently unidentified.

Digital Signature Signing Process and the Scrolls

Decades after the scrolls and scroll fragments were photographed, and years after they were digitized for computerized research, a team of technicians conducted a Digital Signature Signing Process (DSP) of the scrolls and fragments. What is DSP? DSP handles batches of digital image files one file at a time and produces a unique digital signature of each file. Technicians may conduct DSP for all types of digital files, including maps, historical documents, photographs, and medical, legal, and financial records. DSP is very different from electronic signatures that are used by agencies, corporations, and other establishments. Rather, DSP uses military-grade, asymmetric cryptography that is statistically unforgeable.

In a world where digital information can be easily accessed and altered, it is essential to protect the original content from unauthorized changes, whether the changes are malicious, intentional, or inadvertent. DSP provides a process for the owner, or archivist, of a digital asset to preserve the exact content of the asset at a given moment in time. The digital signature of each file may be validated at any later time in order to authenticate that the integrity of the original content has been maintained in an archive. Any subsequent changes to the asset content may easily be detected by regenerating the digital signature. The DSP files of the scrolls are now stored in a university library vault.

Multispectral Imaging

In recent years, scholars have used an "intriguing new digital imaging technology" that

> is unveiling previously illegible and even unseen text on ancient manuscripts recovered from caves near the Dead Sea, the ashes of Vesuvius, and

Steven and Susan Booras conduct multispectral imaging on the Herculaneum scrolls at the Biblioteca Nazionale di Napoli (the National Library of Naples, Italy, 2000).

the ruins of Petra. Known as multispectral imaging (MSI), the technology has outperformed conventional photographic techniques in many applications, capturing images that are shedding new light on history. This initial success at producing superior textual images of fragile, deteriorating antiquities—and electronically preserving those images for future study and appreciation—has attracted widespread interest and bodes well for the continued use of MSI technology in archaeological fieldwork.[5]

These images illustrate the value of multispectral imaging in revealing text that was previously not visible. The scroll PHerc 1669 before multispectral imaging (*above*) and after (*below*).

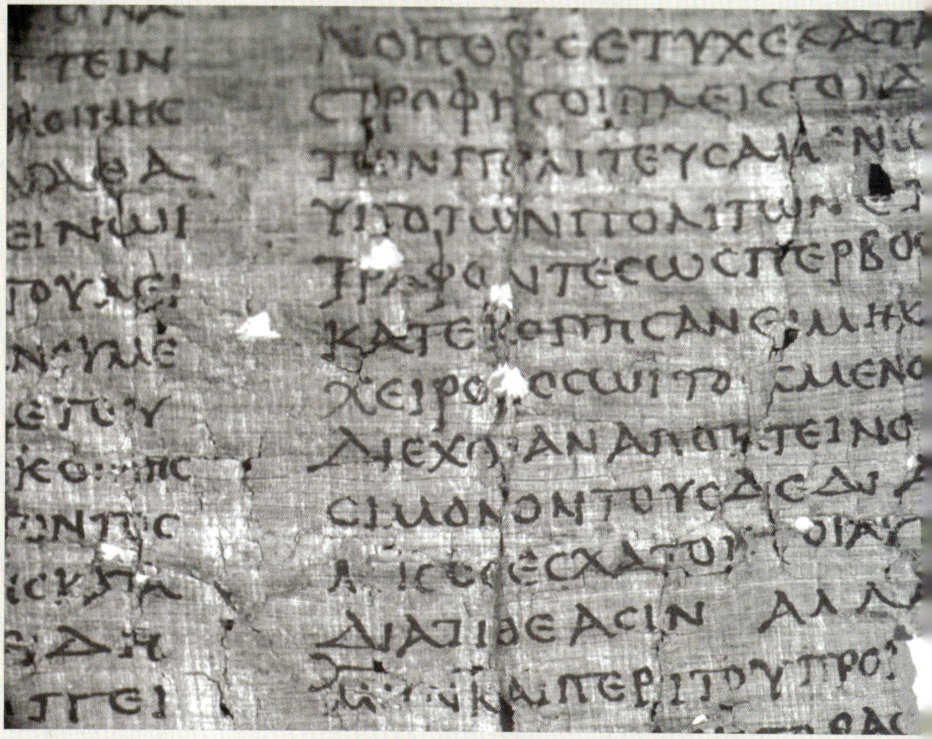

Nonliterary Writings

Practicing the ABCs

In 1953, archaeologist Roland de Vaux discovered an ostracon (broken piece of an earthen jar) slightly north of the Qumran settlement. The ostracon features a portion of the jar's handle and, more significantly, four lines of Hebrew writing. The writing, scholars learned, was an abecedary, or an inscription setting forth the ABCs (but in Hebrew). A child, a youth, or perhaps a scribe, practiced the ABCs on this ostracon. In English, line three would look like this: "a a b c d e f g h." The one who wrote those letters wrote *a* twice, followed by the letters *b* through *h*. The other three lines of writing contain random letters.

Multiple examples of abecedaries were discovered in the caves of the Judaean Desert, including the one above on which someone practiced the ABCs.

The World of Business and Commerce— Two Thousand Years Ago

Notwithstanding that most Dead Sea Scrolls constitute religious compositions of one type or another, a number

Two inkwells discovered at Qumran.

of scroll fragments comprise nonliterary documents, such as business instruments or legal agreements. Examples include bills of marriage and divorce, a "waiver of claims given by a woman to her divorced husband, a receipt for dates, a tiny fragment—perhaps a ketubbah, a fragment of a deed dealing with deposits, one promissory note (in Hebrew), a few fragments of accounts, and one letter (in Hebrew) addressed to Shim'on son of Kosibah."[1] Some documents were written by scribes; others by nonprofessionals. Most nonliterary documents are inscribed in Hebrew or Aramaic on papyrus, although both Greek and Nabataean are also used.

These documents may include one or more of the following elements: the date, place, parties involved, type of sale, property description, sum, receipt, ownership, guarantee, exchange of the deed, signatures of the buyer and seller, and signatures of the witnesses. Depending on the nature of the document, the signatures are written on the front or back. Proper names attested in the documents include the female names Sarah, Shalam, and Shlamsion; male names include

Many nonliterary writings were discovered in various caves of the Judaean Desert, including this document that refers to cereals and legumes.

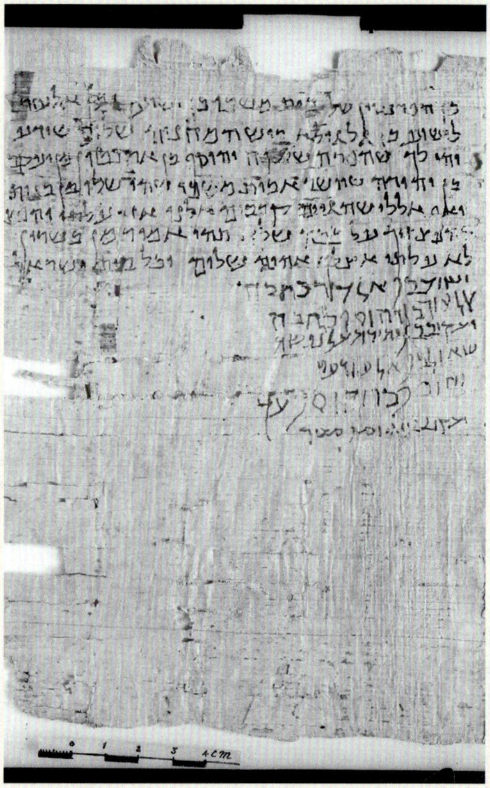

A letter written on a sheet of papyrus. Note the signatures under the body of the letter.

Nonliterary Writings

El'azar, Yehuda, Yehonathan, Yehosef, and Shim'on.

The nonliterary documents have increased our knowledge considerably regarding business practices and the nature of legal agreements during the decades before the Christian era.

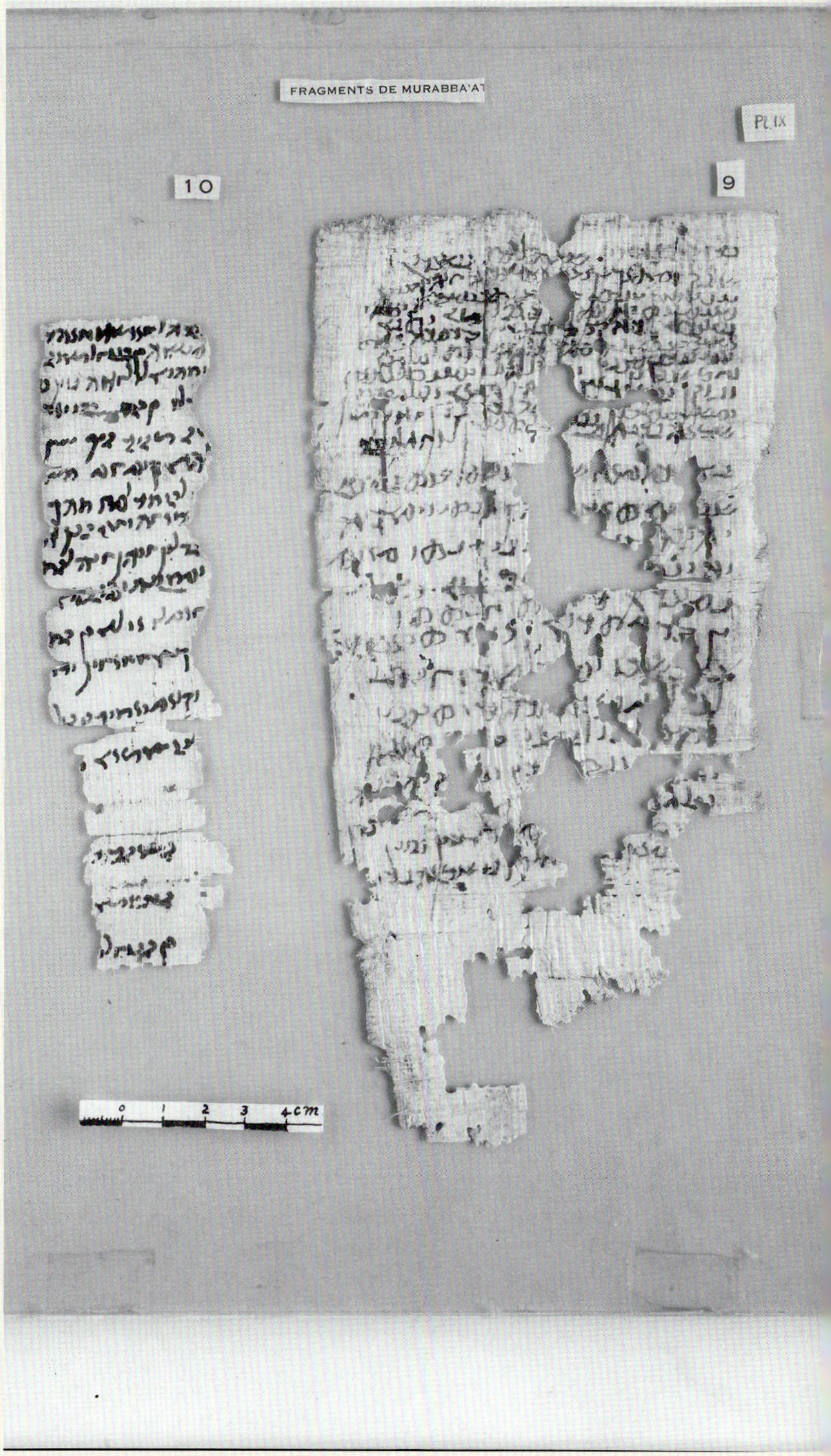

A writ of divorce appears on the left of this image. On the right is a contract of marriage written in Aramaic on papyrus. The signatures of the contract (not shown) are written on the back side.

Notes

Chapter 1

1. John Trever, *The Untold Story of the Dead Sea Scrolls* (Westood, NJ: Revell, 1965), 22.
2. Trever, *Untold Story*, 43.
3. Trever, *Untold Story*, 60.
4. Trever, *Untold Story*, 85.
5. Emanuel Tov, foreword to DJD XIII, ix.
6. For a comprehensive list of scrolls classified according to content and genre, see Armin Lange with Ulrike Mittmann-Richert, "Annotated List of the Texts from the Judaean Desert Classified by Content and Genre," in DJD XXXIX, 115–64.

Chapter 2

1. "Within the Qumran corpus of some 900 texts, the *c.*200 biblical texts constitute 22% (not counting the *tefillin* and *mezuzot*)." Emanuel Tov, "Categorized List of the 'Biblical Texts,'" in DJD XXXIX, 167.
2. For a listing of biblical texts discovered among the scrolls, see Eugene Ulrich, "An Index of the Passages in the Biblical Manuscripts from the Judean Desert (Genesis–Kings)," *Dead Sea Discoveries* 1/1 (1994): 113–29; and Eugene Ulrich, "An Index of the Passages in the Biblical Manuscripts from the Judean Desert (Part 2: Isaiah–Chronicles)," *Dead Sea Discoveries* 2/1 (1995): 86–107.
3. Hosea, Joel, Amos, Obadiah, Jonah, Micah, Nahum, Habakkuk, Zephaniah, Haggai, Zechariah, and Malachi.
4. Tov, "Categorized List of the 'Biblical Texts,'" 167–76.
5. Harold P. Scanlin, *The Dead Sea Scrolls and Modern Translations of the Old Testament* (Wheaton, IL: Tyndale House, 1993), 27.
6. Martin Abegg, Peter Flint, and Eugene Ulrich, trans., *The Dead Sea Scrolls Bible* (San Francisco: Harper, 1999).
7. For a discussion of views regarding John and Qumran, see Florentino García Martínez and Julio Trebolle Barrera, *The People of the Dead Sea Scrolls: Their Writings, Beliefs and Practices*, trans. Wilfred G. E. Watson (Leiden: Brill, 1995), 205–6.
8. Rule of the Community V, 13–14; see also IV, 20–21, in Geza Vermes, trans., *The Complete Dead Sea Scrolls in English* (New York: Penguin Press, 1997), 104, 103.
9. Emanuel Tov, *Textual Criticism of the Hebrew Bible*, 3rd ed. (Minneapolis: Fortress Press, 2011).

Chapter 3

1. Genesis Apocryphon XX, 2–10, in Vermes, *Complete Dead Sea Scrolls*, 454.
2. Genesis Apocryphon XX, 18–30, in Vermes, *Complete Dead Sea Scrolls*, 455.
3. Genesis Apocryphon XXI, 8–22, in Vermes, *Complete Dead Sea Scrolls*, 456.

4. Temple Scroll XXIX, 8–10, in Vermes, *Complete Dead Sea Scrolls*, 200.
5. Yigael Yadin, *The Temple Scroll*, 3 vols. (Jerusalem: IES, Institute of Archaeology of the Hebrew University of Jerusalem, and the Shrine of the Book, 1983), 1:390–92, 396–97.
6. The Seductress, in Vermes, *Complete Dead Sea Scrolls*, 395.
7. The Seductress, in Vermes, *Complete Dead Sea Scrolls*, 396.
8. The Seductress, in Vermes, *Complete Dead Sea Scrolls*, 395.
9. The Seductress, in Vermes, *Complete Dead Sea Scrolls*, 396.
10. Johann Meier, "Wiles of the Wicked Woman," in *Encyclopedia of the Dead Sea Scrolls*, ed. Lawrence H. Schiffman and James C. VanderKam (Oxford: Oxford University Press, 2000), 2:976.
11. Beatitudes II, in Vermes, *Complete Dead Sea Scrolls*, 424.
12. Messianic Apocalypse, in Vermes, *Complete Dead Sea Scrolls*, 391–92.
13. Émile Puech, "Messianic Apocalypse," in *Encyclopedia of the Dead Sea Scrolls*, 1:543.
14. An Account of David's Poems, in Vermes, *Complete Dead Sea Scrolls*, 307.
15. Hymn to the Creator XXVI, 10–13, in Vermes, *Complete Dead Sea Scrolls*, 306.
16. Apostrophe to Zion XXII, 1–9, in Vermes, *Complete Dead Sea Scrolls*, 305–6.
17. See especially the following publications: Eugene Ulrich, "The Notion and Definition of Canon," in *The Canon Debate*, ed. Lee Martin McDonald and James A. Sanders (Peabody, MA: Hendrickson, 2002), 21–35; Philip R. Davies, "The Jewish Scriptural Canon in Cultural Perspective," in *Canon Debate*, 36–52; Joseph Blenkinsopp, "The Formation of the Hebrew Bible Canon: Isaiah as a Test Case," in *Canon Debate*, 53–67; and Lee Martin McDonald, *The Biblical Canon: Its Origin, Transmission, and Authority* (Peabody, MA: Hendrickson, 2007). See also the bibliographies cited in these publications.
18. Tov, "Categorized List of the 'Biblical Texts,'" 166.
19. James C. VanderKam, "Questions of Canon Viewed through the Dead Sea Scrolls," in *Canon Debate*, 91.
20. VanderKam, "Questions of Canon," 92.
21. VanderKam, "Questions of Canon," 108.
22. On the topic of the Dead Sea Scrolls and the canon of scripture, see the discussion in James C. VanderKam, *The Dead Sea Scrolls Today* (Grand Rapids, MI: Eerdmans, 1994), 142–44, 149, 157.
23. Abegg, Flint, and Ulrich, *Dead Sea Scrolls Bible*, xvii.
24. VanderKam, "Questions of Canon," 109.

Chapter 4

1. Pliny, *Natural History* 5.15.73.
2. Vermes, *Complete Dead Sea Scrolls*, 163.
3. War Scroll (1QM) I, in Vermes, *Complete Dead Sea Scrolls*, 163–64.
4. War Scroll XII, in Vermes, *Complete Dead Sea Scrolls*, 175.
5. War Scroll XII, in Vermes, *Complete Dead Sea Scrolls*, 175.
6. War Scroll I, in Vermes, *Complete Dead Sea Scrolls*, 163–64.
7. War Scroll X–XI, in Vermes, *Complete Dead Sea Scrolls*, 173–74.
8. Thanksgiving Hymn 5, in Vermes, *Complete Dead Sea Scrolls*, 249.

9. MMT (4Q398 14–17 ii conflated with 4Q399), in Vermes, *Complete Dead Sea Scrolls*, 228.
10. Rule of the Community VII, 4–14, in Vermes, *Complete Dead Sea Scrolls*, 107–8.
11. The New Jerusalem (4Q554–55), in Vermes, *Complete Dead Sea Scrolls*, 569.
12. The New Jerusalem (5Q15), in Vermes, *Complete Dead Sea Scrolls*, 569.

Chapter 5

1. Vermes, *Complete Dead Sea Scrolls*, 357.
2. Vermes, *Complete Dead Sea Scrolls*, 357.
3. 4QHoroscope (4Q186), fr. i, col. III, in Vermes, *Complete Dead Sea Scrolls*, 358.
4. Copper Scroll I, 1–10, in Vermes, *Complete Dead Sea Scrolls*, 585.
5. Moses H. Segal, "El, Elohim, and YHWH in the Bible," *Jewish Quarterly Review* 46 (1995): 100.
6. García Martínez and Trebolle Barrera, *People of the Dead Sea Scrolls*, 194.
7. For a complete study on scribal marks and notations, see Emanuel Tov, "Scribal Notations in the Texts from the Judaean Desert," in DJD XXXIX, 323–50.

Chapter 6

1. Frank Moore Cross, "The Development of the Jewish Scripts," in *The Bible and the Ancient Near East: Essays in Honor of William Foxwell Albright*, ed. G. Ernest Wright (Garden City: Anchor Books, 1965), 136.
2. See chart in Lawrence H. Schiffman, *Reclaiming the Dead Sea Scrolls* (Philadelphia: Jewish Publication Society, 1994), 32–33.
3. Emanuel Tov, ed., *The Dead Sea Scrolls Electronic Reference Library* (Leiden: Brill, 1999).
4. Scott R. Woodward et al. "Analysis of Parchment Fragments from the Judean Desert Using DNA Techniques," in *Current Research and Technological Developments on the Dead Sea Scrolls: Conference on the Texts from the Judean Desert, Jerusalem, 30 April 1995*, ed. Donald W. Parry and Stephen D. Ricks (Leiden: Brill, 1996), 216.
5. Douglas M. Chabries, Steven W. Booras, and Gregory H. Bearman, "Imaging the Past: Recent Applications of Multispectral Imaging Technology to Deciphering Manuscripts," *Antiquity: A Quarterly Review of Archaeology* 77 (June 2003): 2.

Chapter 7

1. DJD XXVII, 9.

Photo Credits

Brigham Young University, courtesy of the Biblioteca Nazionale, Naples, Italy: page 81 (PHerc 1669).

Donald W. Parry: pages viii, 27 (col. 46), 70, 74, 76, 78.

Garo Nalbandian: page 69 (Copper Scrolls strips).

Hershel Shanks/Biblical Archaeology Society, Washington, DC; www.biblicalarchaeology.org: pages 18, 69 (Cave 3).

Israel Antiquities Authority, Photo Tslia Sagiv, Shai Halevi, Courtesy Israel Antiquities Authority: pages 8, 9, 14 (table-like structures), 23, 24–25, 27 (Job, Exodus), 32, 40, 42, 44 (Words of Moses, Birth of Noah), 50, 58, 62, 63, 65, 66, 71, 75, 83, 84, (cereals and legumes, letter), 85.

Jared Pfost: page 38.

Jason B. Jones: page 73.

Jed B. Jones: page 11 (Dead Sea).

John C. Trever, PhD, digital image by James E. Trever: pages 2, 3, 4 (Metropolitan), 5 (Muhammed group, Trever), 6, 14 (scriptorium), 19 (Metropolitan), 31, 34, 43.

Mark A. Philbrick/BYU Photo: page 80.

Mindy Jeppesen: pages ix, back cover.

Shutterstock/ChameleonsEye: pages x, 11 (cave 4, exterior), 16, 41; Lukas Hlavac: page 1 (warrior); Jose Ignacio Soto: page 1 (Tutankhamun mask); Dimos: page 1 (Petra); Aprilphoto: page 13; Joseph Calev: page 20; Konstantnin: page 22; Magdalena Kucova: page 29; SeanPavonePhoto: page 33; Anneka: page 36; David Rafael Moulis, page 54; LHF Graphics: page 79.

Steven W. Booras and Donald W. Parry: page 35.

Wall Street Journal, Tuesday, June 1, 1954: page 19.

West Semitic Research, Bruce and Kenneth Zuckerman. Courtesy Department of Antiquities, Jordan: page 69 (Copper Scroll close-up).

Zev Radovan/BibleLandPictures.com: pages front cover, ii, 4 (jars), 11 (Cave 4, interior; Cave 11), 12, 15 (stairs, cistern), 21, 46, 82.